IT STARTED WITH A GREEN LINE BUS

Boyhood in Harpenden

before and during

The Second World War

Ralph Webster

The Book Castle

DEDICATION

This book is dedicated to the memory of
Alan Bell (9.3.28 to 11.1.98), a fellow
pupil at Moreton End, and a life-long friend

First published August 2003
by
The Book Castle
12 Church Street
Dunstable
Bedfordshire LU5 4RU

© Ralph Webster, 2003

The right of Ralph Webster to be identified as the Author of this work has been asserted by him in accordance with the Copyright, Designs and Patents Act, 1988.

ISBN 1 903747 37 6

Designed and typeset by Caroline and Roger Hillier
The Old Chapel Graphic Design

Printed by Grillford, Granby, Milton Keynes

Contents

ABOUT THE AUTHOR

Ralph Webster was born in Harpenden in 1928 and lived in the "village" until 1993 when he retired to Dorset with his wife Delma. In March 2001 they celebrated their golden wedding anniversary. Their two sons, Henry and Barnaby, still live in Harpenden.

Ralph attended Victoria Road school from 1933 to 1936 when he moved to Moreton End School (now renamed Harpenden Preparatory School).

In 1939 at the outbreak of the Second World War, his father moved the family to stay with relatives in Derbyshire whilst he returned to Harpenden to close down his building firm of H.E. Webster for the duration of the War. His father then obtained employment in Bedford, attached to The Royal Engineers, but in a civilian capacity as deputy commander.

Meanwhile, the author's education in Derbyshire was almost non-existent. There was no attendance at school, teaching being carried out by correspondence. Work was taken in weekly for marking and a new task collected for the following week – without any contact with a teacher whatsoever. This went on for six months until the return to Harpenden when Ralph was sent to St. Albans Modern School. Nowadays this is better known as Verulam School. Having spent two years there, he was next sent to Bedford School, where he completed his education in 1945. In September of that year he joined his father's firm which had resumed business after its closure for the duration of the war. Today, the company is still flourishing, and is located in the Batford area of Harpenden. Having completed six years with his father, he joined the multi-national company of George Wimpey, first as a junior quantity surveyor, eventually retiring in 1989 as the chief estimator for his department's private development estates.

Now, in retirement, Ralph is able to enjoy his garden, and pursue one of his favourite pastimes – watching cricket.

For this book the author draws upon his personal collection of photographs, but also acknowledges with thanks those passed to him by his late brother Brian, and to the London Transport Museum for permission to use the pictures on the front and back covers. Thanks are also passed to Paul Bowes and Sally Siddons of the Book Castle in Dunstable for their help in putting the book together for publication.

"Buddies"

The author (right) outside No.24 Willoughby Road with his friend, Donald
Chell, in 1931. (The wrought iron gates were taken down when war was
declared, and melted down to help build tanks.)

INTRODUCTION

'It started with a Green Line Bus' describes life in Harpenden during the 1930s, including the period leading to the outbreak of the Second World War. It also covers the years during the war, and the immediate post war days after peace was achieved in 1945.

For the first seven years of his life the author lived in Willoughby Road which was not considered to be one of the better areas of Harpenden. Later, in 1936, he moved with his family to Bowers House, one of the oldest Harpenden houses in Lower High Street, now sadly hidden from view by Bowers Parade. Another notable house, Wellington House in Leyton Road, also features in the book. The tranquillity of living in such a house is portrayed vividly, including a visit to one of his school friends in Milton Road where he remembers crystal lemonade being served by the resident maid.

The plethoric abundance of schools is also recalled. The book describes the snobbishness which then existed and meant that parents felt obliged to find a private school for their sons and daughters instead of sending them to the Local Council school (the forerunner of today's state school). Harpenden residents not only reflected on the school for their offspring but also felt it imperative to keep abreast of their neighbours in the status of their house, where you lived, and your employment. All these factors were taken into account in marking your position in social standing, and in guarding your own independence.

The book describes the author's boyhood experiences as a pupil at Moreton End School (renamed Harpenden Preparatory School in 1995), founded seventy years ago with only five boys.

Older readers will no doubt recall the various High Street shops in the 1930s and 1940s remembered by the author. Life during the war is also recollected – the local Home Guard, rationing, enemy air attacks, and the bravery of the sons of Harpenden during this period.

This book will appeal not only to those local inhabitants who can still call to mind this time in their lives, but also to newcomers who will be interested to learn of life which existed in Harpenden during the 1930s and 1940s.

CHAPTER ONE

A Revelation

"Try to speak a little nicer!"

This was the first time in my life I was aware that some form of class distinction existed in Harpenden or, for that matter, anywhere.

It was 1936 and my first day at Moreton End School.

Although I was not quite eight years old, I somehow felt that my childhood was over and that I was moving into an adult world.

At that age, in those times, it was not considered 'manly' to be escorted to school by your parents so I had dutifully reported at Moreton End by myself on the first day of the Easter term.

I had been introduced to the Headmaster, Mr Vic H Card, by his wife, Vera, who had met me at the front entrance of the Victorian building in Luton Road at the northern end of Harpenden. Mrs Card was of smallish to medium height with short, Eton-cropped dark hair; was well-manicured and wore a dark two-piece costume. She was thirty-eight years of age, a small Yorkshire terrier at her heels. She spoke with a clipped B.B.C. Announcer accent.

"In future," she said, "you will come into school by the back entrance."

This, I had already observed, was a wooden gate let into the fence facing Moreton End Lane.

"Now go and take your place for Assembly. I'll show you where to go."

She led the way into the largest room on the ground floor which had a large window facing the rear garden, and another facing Moreton End Lane to the side. This had no doubt once been the drawing room when the building had been used as a private residence, but now looked very austere. The colour brown dominated the entire room; brown wall panelling, brown forms to sit on, and brown desks which had been pushed to the back of the room so that the entire school assembly could be accommodated.

Mr Card took up his position behind a desk at the front of the room and gave the appearance of an emperor behind his podium. He was a fairly well-built man, dark, unsmiling, and probably thirty-two or thirty-three years of age. He wore a well-cut dark suit and spoke with a neutral, standard English accent – the kind favoured by modern newsreaders.

The teaching staff, Mr Macdonald, Mr Buckingham and Miss Edwards, took up their places sitting in chairs which had been placed behind the Headmaster. Both Mr Macdonald and Mr Buckingham were in their late twenties. Mr Macdonald, the French master, in blazer, worsted flannels, old school tie of uncertain origin, and with sleeked fair hair, was inclined to be rather effeminate. Mr Buckingham, with thinning red hair also sleeked back, was wearing a dark suit. Both looked slim and fit. Indeed, both took the boys for various sports activities. Miss

Edwards was dark with her hair drawn back in a bun and wearing an old-fashioned dress – yet was probably no more than twenty-five years of age.

There were thirty-four boys in the school and I was the only new boy that Easter term. Of the thirty-four, six boys boarded.

"Welcome to the new term," began Mr Card, who then proceeded to tell the "parable of the talents". I was later to discover that each new term began with this parable; this would link to the cup inscribed "TO HIM THAT OVERCOMETH". One recipient of this cup was a boy named Hawkes, very nervous at first, almost afraid of games, later a Cambridge rowing blue. This same boy, Michael Hawkes, was also to become the Deputy Chairman of Kleinwort Benson, the well-known merchant bankers.

Assembly finished with a hymn and I took my place in the classroom on the third floor at the very top of the house, with Miss Edwards presiding. The room was surprisingly large for what once must have been occupied by a servant. The school itself was housed in a three-storey semi-detached Victorian building and was huge. The other half of the semi was comparatively small, only two storeys in height and called "Moreton Lodge". It appeared to disassociate itself from the school next door. Even after almost seventy years, little seems to have changed.

Miss Edwards took up a piece of chalk and commenced the lesson, writing something on the blackboard.

I put my hand up.

"Please, miss, I can't read joined-up writing." I had arrived at Moreton End full of confidence in myself, but for the first time a few doubts began to enter my mind. Perhaps my scholastic achievements were not as advanced as I thought.

Miss Edwards was surprisingly sympathetic and supportive. "I'll print on the blackboard for your benefit." And so she did. It was to be half term before I was able to read joined-up handwriting.

At the end of the lesson, we all filed out to go to French on the next floor down. This would be taken by Mr Macdonald.

French. A completely new subject for me but, as I recollect, I quite enjoyed my first lesson. We were all lining up to go to Maths, which would be taken by Mr Card himself, when Mr Macdonald took me to one side.

"Webster, " he said.

"Yes, sir?"

"Try to speak a little nicer!"

I was dumbfounded. What was wrong with the way I spoke? It seemed to be the same as everybody else. I had no impediment in my speech. What on earth could Mr Macdonald mean? I simply had no means of being aware that, having spent almost three years at Victoria Road School, the local council elementary school (now occupied by Harpenden Community Education Centre), I had acquired a rough 'Hertfordshire' accent – not, apparently, favoured by Moreton End.

"I don't know what you mean, sir."

"Well, listen to the other boys and try to copy them."

My first awareness that some form of class snobbishness existed in Harpenden. So much for the "parable of the talents" which I'd listened to at assembly!

In the 1930s, parents strove to send their children to a private school. Consequently, a plethora of this type of school grew in Harpenden and I recall a few of them:

St Hilda's School Originally founded in 1890 in Rothamsted Avenue and later transferred to Douglas Road where it still exists today.

Hardenwick Moved in 1898 to the site bounded by Townsend Road and Wordsworth Road. The site was sold for private housing in the late 1960s and the school moved to Sandridgebury but was later disbanded altogether.

Walton House School A kindergarten at 18, Tennyson Road.

Lee House School Opened in 1937 by the late Kenneth Castle as Headmaster. Moved to Aldwickbury in 1948 and changed its name to Aldwickbury.

St Dominic's Moved from Harpenden Hall to "Welcome House" in 1931. This school moved further southwards along Southdown Road to its present site in 1964 when Welcome House was sold to become the Moat House Hotel. Over £600,000 was spent on converting Welcome House into a hotel before it opened for business on 6th October 1972.

St George's School Originally founded in 1887 by the Rev R H Wix but rented by the Rev Cecil Grant in 1907 for his Keswick Co-educational School.
For many years, a sign at the school entrance off Carlton Road proclaimed "For the sons and daughters of Gentlemen".

Moreton End Opened with five boys in 1933 by Mr V E H Card who formerly had been the Maths teacher at Hardenwick School. In the 1990s, Moreton End School was re-named The Harpenden Preparatory School.

In the 1930s, the total population of Harpenden was only 9,000 but all these private schools thrived because, if parents sent their child to the Council School, they were pigeon-holed as "working class" or even "lower working class"; this was simply not good enough for those who considered themselves to be "middle" or "upper" class. This was indeed another form of "keeping up with the Jones's" and very prevalent in Harpenden in those days.

There were many who thought that the posh, overpost version of standard English – the Prince of Wales accent, the old-fashioned Eton and Harrow accent – would open the doors to success. Fifty years ago they were right. Today it no longer does so and probably cuts you off. A good thing too.

At break on my first day, I almost collided with a boy on the first floor landing. "Hello," he said, "I'm Bell." I told him my name.

We remained the best of friends until his untimely death in January 1998, but on that first morning he made me feel that I was not alone in my new school. I had a friend.

CHAPTER TWO

From Small Beginnings

I had led, I suppose, a fairly idyllic life in my infancy and childhood before starting at Moreton End School. No particular worries, no pressures of competitiveness with other children, either academic or in sports (although I remember how pleased my father was when I won a race for 7-year olds on Harpenden Common during the 1935 Silver Jubilee celebrations).

Competition in designer-label clothes simply did not exist; neither did it with the type of car that your father drove; very few people had a car.

In 1925, my parents had moved southwards from Derbyshire after their marriage on 25th October. They lived initially in rented accommodation at Redbourn and my father cycled daily to work in Harpenden. He had secured a position as a draughtsman for a small building firm, Poate & Thornton, which had a small office in Townsend Lane.

By 1928, my father had gone into partnership with a Mr Harvey who lived in Luton. The building firm of Harvey & Webster acquired a yard in Willoughby Road and my father also rented a semi-detached house a few doors away at Number 24. Harvey & Webster also acquired a piece of land at the bottom of Kirkdale Road on which they built a small office. It was single storey, brick built and rendered and painted white on the front. The name of Harvey & Webster was added to the fascia. This office is presently used by Jackson (plumbing suppliers).

On 28th June 1928, I was born.

My earliest memory is being taken for a walk over the fields from Batford to Sauncey Wood, not by my parents but by their maid, Nancy, who had travelled from Newcastle to obtain employment. I think she was paid fifteen shillings (75p) per week, plus her keep. It did not occur to me that there was anything unusual in employing a maid at a semi-detached house. I daresay that this was not uncommon at the beginning of the 1930s decade and, I suppose, another instance of keeping up with the Jones's. However, I do not recall anyone else in Willoughby Road having a maid.

Nancy was a fresh-faced young girl, quite strict with me but inclined to take liberties with my parents' things when they were out. After a couple of years, she left. I never really found out why, although I heard whispered snatches of conversation between my mother and my aunt that she had been caught trying on my mother's clothes. I also heard my aunt whispering that this had been with my father's permission. All conversation seemed to end abruptly when they realised I was in earshot. Anyhow, the girl left and some years later married a baker from Ackroyd's Bakery. For a number of years, I saw her in Harpenden with her husband and family, then she disappeared.

Of course, Batford today and the hill up to Sauncey Wood are

Beginnings in Kirkdale Road

Office at the bottom of Kirkdale Road in 1932. Harvey & Webster acquired the site in 1930, and the single storey office was built in the same year. It was staffed by a young clerk (Ron Tansley) complete with candlestick telephone and trumpet earpiece.

occupied by the Council Housing Estate but in the early 1930s the hill was just fields, sometimes set with wheat but mostly left to grass so that a young toddler would be walking amid tall grasses almost as big as himself. I remember on a summer's day, lying in the grass halfway up the hill, looking up at the blue sky and feeling very content with life.

Between 1920 and 1930, the population of Harpenden remained fairly constant at 7,000 people in 1920 to around 9,000 in 1930. These were wealthy bankers, stockbrokers, and industrialists who lived in the large houses in 'The Avenues' district and also in 'The Poets' area (Milton Road, Spenser Road, Cowper Road and Shakespeare Road) which were conveniently located near to the station for daily commuting to London. In 1930, the season ticket rates to St Pancras from Harpenden were:

First Class, three months £8.8s.9d. (£8.44)
Third Class, three months £5.9s.3d. (£5.46)
Third Class, weekly 11/6d (57 pence)
Cheap tickets daily inc. return 3/2d (16 pence)

All trains were steam driven and the fastest journey to St Pancras took thirty-five minutes. The average 'slow' train took an hour.

At this period, there were no less than 1,400 season ticket holders. The geographical position of Harpenden was then, and still is, very convenient for businessmen.

Although, by now, motor omnibuses plied between Harpenden and the outlying villages, it was still possible to use a horse and brougham 'taxi' service from Harpenden Station. I remember

Taxi Sir?
The horse-drawn taxi which used to wait at Harpenden Station (partly shown on the right of the picture). Mr. Hogg ran this service until 1936. Many passengers only used the service as a last resort thinking it unseemly to be seen by their friends in this mode of transport, and consequently used to crouch down to avoid recognition.

seeing this very Victorian-looking entrepreneur, complete with top hat, who operated this service from the 1920s until just before the war. He used to meet the evening trains in Station Approach and, sitting up top, conveyed those who availed themselves in his 'taxi' to their houses.

Our garden at No. 24, Willoughby Road was quite long, and right at the bottom an embankment carried the railway track which led from Harpenden East Station to Luton. This small branch line also took passengers in the other direction to Welwyn

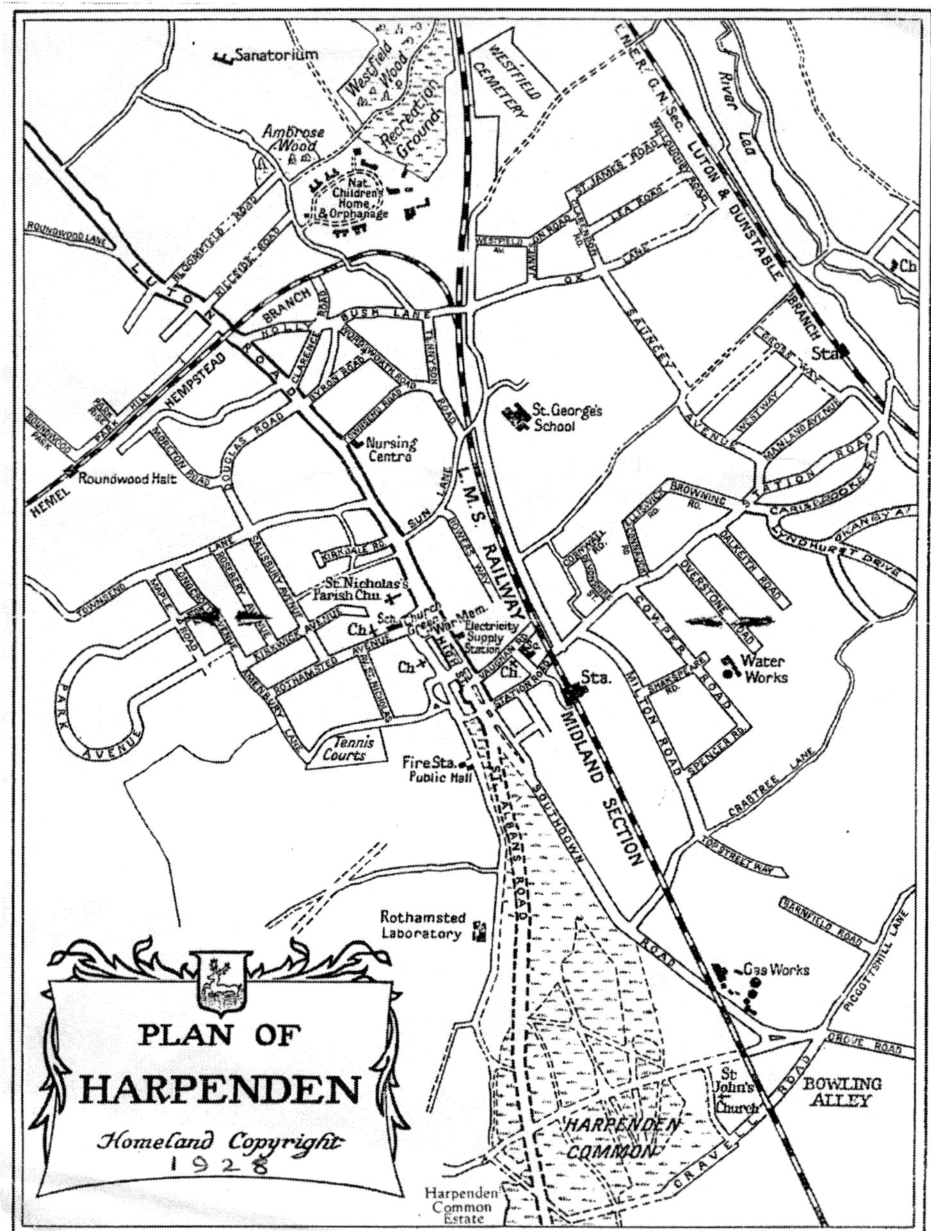

Plan of Harpenden in 1928
Some areas of Harpenden were as yet still undeveloped.

via Wheathampstead. The two or three carriages were pulled by a small steam engine which puffed its way at a very sedate pace along the track. The station and branch line disappeared at the time of Dr Beeching's economy cuts and today the area where the station used to be sited is occupied by the offices of Messrs. Jarvis Construction Company.

Another early memory is of the long garden in Willoughby Road. One day, I was supposed to be helping my father to make a bonfire. Suddenly he called out, "Look, there's the R101" and he was pointing to the sky. I looked up and saw the cylindrical airship sedately crossing, almost imperceptibly moving across the sky. It became more poignant to me the following day when my father gave me the news that the R101 had crashed after crossing the English Channel. There were no survivors.

At No. 28 lived the Mardell family. The father, Henry, worked as a gardener for a wealthy family at Mackeryend and cycled to work each day. He was painfully thin and wore round 'pebble' spectacles. His wife was the most hardworking woman I ever knew. She had borne seven children – three boys and four girls – and had to work with quite primitive equipment. Not for her the luxury of an automatic washing machine or spin dryer; no refrigerator or central heating. These things simply did not exist as we know them today. She was plump and suffered from heart trouble. She wore herself out, poor soul, and died in her early fifties: her like is not seen today.

As was the case with the father's name, all the children were given plain old English names: Roy, Ted, Anthony, Elsie (but always called Chibby), Betty, Jean and Pamela. In those days, I don't think people ever contemplated calling their children

Darryl, Tracy, or Sharon, Wayne, Sandra or Pippa. These are very much names of today.

The family did not have much money. The father's pay seemed barely enough on which to keep his large family and Henry had to cultivate an allotment on a piece of land almost opposite and adjoining Lea Road on its northern side. Being a natural and keen gardener, I'm sure he enjoyed it, and many years later he was able to buy his allotment land. This undoubtedly was a good investment because he was able to sell it eventually for housing development, and today a pair of houses stands on the site (Nos.47/49 Lea Road).

I recollect that Mr and Mrs Mardell were extremely good neighbours to my parents. Mrs Mardell did odd jobs for my mother (God knows how she found the time) and was always helpful with advice on bringing up children. Later, Ted sometimes took me to school.

The atmosphere in Willoughby Road in those days was, I should imagine, similar to that which prevailed in the East End of London where there were rows upon rows of terraced houses. The doors were never locked and neighbours used to call in at will, perhaps to borrow something or offer some help, or merely for a gossip. Nowadays, people would expect you to telephone first; they are too jealous of their own independence.

I recently met Ted and he told me that after his father's death some twenty years ago, the youngest daughter, Pamela, bought the house at No. 28, Willoughby Road, and still lives there.

Our neighbours on the other side, at No. 22, Willoughby Road, were Mr and Mrs Bent who lived there with their son and daughter, Bert and Dorrie. Bert was good at running and showed

Good Neighbours

Brother and sister Roy and "Chibby" Mardell in 1940, both in uniform (R.A.F.);
the picture was taken at the bottom of their garden No.28 Willoughby Road.

me his spiked running shoes. I had never seen a pair before. Dorrie worked as a shop assistant in Rowes, the bakers (now *Boswell's Sandwich Bar*). Next to the Bents lived the Goodsons; then came Taylors General Stores, followed by the Gray and Coote families.

When I was about two years old, I developed rickets. In those days it was not uncommon in children between the ages of about the ninth month and third year. It was caused by a deficiency of vitamin D and resulted in a bending of the bones. I became very knock-kneed and was prescribed two forms of treatment by my parents' doctor (Dr Davenport).

Firstly, I had to spend considerable periods of time with my legs bandaged and in leg-irons. Presumably, this was an attempt to straighten my legs. Secondly, I had to visit the Nursing Centre at 40, Luton Road to receive ultra-violet ray lamp treatment. Ultra-violet rays, which can also be found in natural sunlight, act upon the skin and help to form the vitamin D.

Whether or not I was prescribed any other medication to make up for this vitamin deficiency, such as cod liver oil or milk, I cannot remember but I do vaguely recall being given calcium tablets, but perhaps these were to improve the strength of my teeth rather than my bones. Nowadays, rickets is unheard of in England.

Suffice it to say, I hated my treatments. I had to attend the Nursing Centre twice a week and still recall the smell of the goggles and the rubber pantaloons which I had to wear for my sun-ray treatment.

The Nursing Centre was recently demolished. It was used by the National Health Service for weighing and monitoring infants. Originally, it had been a select girls' school called St Helena's

College which opened in 1897. But at the end of the first World War, it was purchased for just £3,000 and, after alterations, became "Harpenden Memorial Nursing Centre" opening in October 1920, being the second part of Harpenden's tribute and memorial to those who gave their lives in the Great War. Every time I go past today, I think of those smelly goggles. Ugh!!

I disliked my leg-irons and bandages because they were so painful, particularly if the bandages were too tight. I still recall being put to bed by my parents one evening and awakening because the bandages were uncomfortable. I called out for my mother, then for my father, but to my horror realised that I was alone in the house. My father had decided to give my mother a break and had taken her out somewhere. I called out as loudly as I could and then went downstairs with difficulty, since my legs were virtually straight due to the leg-irons. Getting downstairs was rather like walking down on stilts. Mrs Bent next door heard my cries and came round to the front door, which I opened. She took me round to her house, removed the leg-iron and undid the bandages. She gave me a hot drink and I remained with her, in her home, until my parents returned later – momentarily distressed to find that I had gone! They never left me alone again.

The Willoughby Road or eastern end of Harpenden was comparatively quiet at the beginning of the 1930s decade. Very little traffic and a fair amount of it was still horse-drawn. Milk used to be delivered by a horse-drawn cart and the daily requirement ladled out into a jug from the silver coloured urns which the cart carried. All coal was delivered by horse-drawn carts. The customers had the option of it being delivered loose – deposited in a heap in the roadway for the householder to barrow in, or the slightly more expensive delivery in sacks, which the coal-man humped onto his back off the cart and then carried them, one by one, down the side passage of the house and deposited the contents into the coal cellar.

In the summertime, the Walls Ice Cream man would come along the road riding his tricycle and ringing the bell, which was fixed to the handlebars. At the front of his tricycle, he carried his cold box container in which his ices were stored. The front of the container held an enamelled notice proclaiming "STOP ME AND BUY ONE". The ice-cream man himself wore a white jacket and blue and white checked trousers, not unlike a chef's uniform. On his head was a straw boater.

My favourite was the "snow fruit" which was, I suppose, the forerunner of today's iced lolly. It cost one penny (in later years, this was increased to two pence or 'tuppence') and was triangular shaped, not unlike a Toblerone chocolate. You could push up the fruit ice inside the cardboard container as you licked it, until eventually you were left with just the soggy remnants of the cardboard wrapping.

Some motorised traffic occasionally came along Willoughby Road, but not much. Consequently, it was very safe for a child to play in the road, and many games were devised and used to take place either on the pavement or in the road itself. "Hopscotch" used to be a favourite game played on the pavement with a grid chalked out and resembling a giant noughts and crosses chart. Another popular game was a form of Tug-o'-War, but this could take place only if the child who owned the rope was present.

One day in May 1931, I thought it a great honour to be taken to the house of an older boy, Peter Woolston, who lived with his mother in one of the large semi-detached houses in Ox Lane, at the corner of its junction with Clarendon Road. Because he was older, I looked on in awe as he produced his possessions, one by one, to show me. It was a sunny morning and eventually he opened a box from which he extracted his prize possession – an air rifle. I spent the next couple of hours happily playing with it under his supervision. Peter was probably at least twelve years old and I was nearly three. I shudder to think how dangerous this might have been but, as children, neither of us sensed any danger.

At lunchtime, I was taken home to 24, Willoughby Road to find that my brother had been born. Dr Davenport and the District Nurse were bathing my new brother when my father took me into the front bedroom. I called out, "Don't put him under the water. He'll drown!" Grins all round. I went downstairs with my father to see Dr Davenport out. The doctor left the nurse still bathing my brother and I felt it my duty to go back up again to supervise that nothing amiss should occur. After all, my mother was in bed and, to my mind, had little control of the situation.

After that, I only saw Peter Woolston on occasions. He joined the R.A.F. when war was declared in 1939 and he became a rear gunner in a bomber air-crew – rather more sophisticated than his air rifle. He lost his life when his aircraft was shot down over the English Channel, and he was last seen parachuting into the sea. Officially, he was reported 'missing' but his mother never believed that he had lost his life. Right up to the time of her own death, she believed that he would return; but, of course, he never did.

I first learned to ride my fairy cycle (the only new bicycle I ever possessed) along Willoughby Road itself. I was then five years of age and it was the summer of 1933.

In those years, it was reasonably safe to allow a child to go out either alone or with friends, and I spent many a happy summer afternoon on a fishing expedition to the River Lea, armed with a fishing net and jam jar.

The walk along Coldharbour Lane to the ford at the bottom of Westfield Road was a favourite. Proceeding from the Ox Lane end, there were old cottages to pass on the left-hand side but, on the other side of the lane, high hedges obscured the view of the fields behind. These fields were bisected by the River Lea.

The lane was quiet and on a summer's day the stillness was broken only by the sounds of insects: perhaps a horsefly, bees or a dragon fly. Once I saw a hornet. Perhaps it was the overgrown hedges which accentuated the narrowness of the lane. Traffic rarely went along and the walk seemed endless, the monotony broken only by the swishing of the wild weeds in the hedgerows with the bamboo of the fishing net. Eventually, you came to the bottom of Westfield Road which stopped at the ford near the Red Cow public house, and a wooden footbridge at the side carried walkers over the ford to emerge at the Lower Luton Road side of the river. A proper road bridge for traffic was not constructed until 1964. Today, the ford at the bottom of Crabtree Lane, near the Marquis of Granby public house, is very similar to how the one at the bottom of Westfield Road looked in the early 1930s.

Occasionally, the fishing venue would be Batford, so the walk along Coldharbour Lane went in the opposite direction after turning right from the bottom of Ox Lane. Again, there were only fields bounded by overgrown hedges on the left-hand side of the lane, and the railway embankment on the right. Nowadays, the fields are occupied by factory units. The walk seemed to take a long time and the lane much narrower than it appears today.

On one summer's day, I went out before lunchtime and decided to go by myself in another direction along Willoughby Road to the field which adjoined Westfield Road (now occupied since the late 1930s by children's swings, roundabouts, etc.). The field had long grasses; soft, warm and gently moving in the slight breeze. I lay down, looking at the blue sky, and soon fell asleep, lulled by the warm sunshine.

I think my eventual return home must have been mid-afternoon and getting on for teatime because I remember arriving back home feeling hungry and being greeted by an anxious mother.

"Where have you been? All the neighbours are out looking for you."

I thought this to be a slight exaggeration because only one neighbour had volunteered to go out to try to find me. Anyway, I wondered, why all the panic? I was completely safe. To a great extent, I suppose, this was completely true in the years of the 1930s decade.

I do not remember seeing all that much of my father in those early days. He seemed to work very hard at his building business and rarely came home before I went to bed. I do recall, however, being taken by him to a fête in the grounds of The Red House in about 1930.

Sir Halley Stewart, the wealthy owner of the London Brick Company at Fletton in Bedfordshire, had bought The Red House in 1904. Sir Halley was a Christian and a philanthropist. When the Rothamsted Estate was for sale, he contributed £500 to Sir John Russell's appeal to buy the Manor House and farm for the

Lawes Agricultural Trust, and "purchased for the village the Manorial Rights of Harpenden Common" at a cost of £2,500 – now vested in Harpenden Town Council, so that the Common is one of the few commons really owned by the people.

In 1929, Sir Halley Stewart made over The Red House to the people of Harpenden so that after his death it should be used as a hospital. He also left one quarter of the cost of necessary alterations, subject to the people of Harpenden raising the remainder. The idea of the fête was to raise funds as a contribution towards the remainder required.

My father and I walked from Willoughby Road into Ox Lane (opposite H.B. Randall's tomato nurseries), then continued up the lane past the high hedges on the left-hand side until we came to Sauncey Avenue where Mr Randall's private residence stood on the corner. This was huge and set in well over one acre of land. (Much of this land has been sold in recent times for residential development and, today, the house remains in much smaller grounds).

We proceeded along Sauncey Avenue and the fields on the left-hand side which, later, were to be the site of Manland School, until we came to the Stewart Road footpath on the right. Stewart Road itself (named after Sir Halley) was only a rough track and not a through road into Sauncey Avenue, as it is today. Not that we had a car so it didn't matter.

I remember that we spent a wonderful afternoon at the fête. There were numerous stalls, clowns, jugglers, gymnasts, magicians, and all the fun of the fair – a really magical afternoon. I remember seeing a waxwork tableau but made up of real people, mostly recognisable shopkeepers. The longer they remained motionless, the more money people gave. I remember seeing Edward (Ted) Bentley, the eldest son of Mr Bentley, the grocer, taking part. He always had a sympathetic feel for a show and indeed appeared in many pantomimes and local stage performances at Harpenden's Public Hall in the 1930s.

Part of The Red House grounds was sold for development in the early 1970s and I often wonder whether this was really what Sir Halley Stewart would have wanted. I somehow feel that he would not, and intended the work of The Red House and grounds to be used as a hospital for the people of Harpenden.

I never really appreciated the long hours my father spent in an endeavour to increase the turnover of his building business. My mother used to tell me that on most nights, he would be at the drawing board preparing plans and specifications, or preparing and pricing estimates for either small works or new houses.

There was a slump in the property business during the Depression of the 1930s, just as there was recently in the 1990s. I remember my father coming home excitedly one Saturday teatime to say that he had sold one of a pair of semi-detached houses near the bottom of Ox Lane. The sale price was £200 which included carpets. He thought himself very astute to have thought up the marketing ploy of including carpets in the sale.

As I have said, the long hours my father worked rather restricted his attention to me. I remember one snowy winter when many of my friends possessed a toboggan, and would reluctantly let me have a ride when I pressed them. I thought it was time I had one of my own and asked my father to make me one. He readily agreed and I expected the finished toboggan to arrive the next day. It didn't. The days went by and the snow still held. Each night I kept awake until I heard my father come in, and then called out, "Is the toboggan ready yet, Dad?" The answer came, "No, I'm still working on it. Now go to sleep."

I assumed that my father was making it after hours in the joiners' shop, after the men had gone home, and there was simply no way I could think of to inspect its progress. Eventually, after about a week, the prized sledge arrived at the back door and I joyously pulled it along the pavement in Willoughby Road. It was still packed with frozen snow. For some reason, I turned in through the gates of the builders' yard and went down to the joinery shop. I suppose I intended showing off the toboggan to the men. There I met my father's foreman, Ernie Russell.

"Oh," he said "Trying out your sledge?"

"Yes," I said "Isn't it a beauty? My dad made it for me."

"Oh, no," replied Ernie, "I made it yesterday; it only took me a few hours."

I was totally disillusioned and, unfortunately, I have never forgotten this incident, in spite of the fact that I always revered, admired and loved my father.

At about this time, I also dreamed of owning a soap box on wheels. Having seen some of my older friends pulling them or riding in them, I craved to possess one. In those days, such a contraption was the home-made version of the modern go-cart, with a long piece of string fixed to the front of the under chassis to act as the steering reins.

I decided to speak to my father about the construction of one. "Well," he said. "If you can find a set of pram wheels, I'll get one made for you," (presumably in the joiners' shop). The problem was, where to find a set of discarded pram wheels, which had to be complete on their chassis? This question taxed me for years. I searched every rubbish tip I could find, hoping that I would come across the prized quest. But I never did and I never got my soapbox on wheels. I even considered whether I could buy one from a friend, but thought I had insufficient money saved in my money-box. Eventually, I grew out of the phase; but when I look around today and see children as young as six years old in possession of a radio-controlled car costing, perhaps, over £100, or a stream-lined manufactured go-cart with a sophisticated steering and braking system, I reflect whimsically on my greatest childish desire – to own a hand-made soap box on wheels costing, at most, a few shillings in those early days of the 1930s decade, and the fact that I never got one!

CHAPTER THREE

Harpenden in the Early 1930s

The day arrived, when I was five years old, to go to school. It was the beginning of September 1933. In those days, nursery or preschool classes did not exist so I had absolutely no idea what to expect. I had some vague notion that it would be fun – simply an extension to the uninhibited life that I had hitherto led. I was soon to be disillusioned!

Apart from the Lindbergh kidnapping case in America which took place in 1934, there were very few cases of child abduction, especially in Great Britain, and unheard of locally. Consequently, children were given much more freedom to come and go as they pleased without parental supervision. Children were packed off to school by themselves with no more warning than, "Don't talk to any gypsies!"

On my first morning at school, my mother walked with me from our home in Willoughby Road, up Ox Lane and into Sun Lane and Carlton Road; then under a railway bridge in Station Road, past the sweet shop which is today occupied by Humbergrove Insurance, and finally up to the corner of Victoria

Road. It had been raining overnight and the pavements were still wet but the sun now shone, with the promise of a fine day.

Outside Ackroyd's baker's shop on the corner (now *Harpenden Grill Kebab*), my mother said to me, "Well, you can find your way from here. You don't want to be seen having your mother take you into school. I'll meet you outside at lunch-time."

I walked along Victoria Road alone, occasionally turning back to see my mother waving outside Ackroyd's. Eventually, I came to the school entrance and went up the steps now used by the Local Education Centre. At the top of the steps I stopped, waited a few minutes, then went down them again and peered round the corner. My mother was nowhere in sight – she had gone home.

Warily, I proceeded along Victoria Road and took a right-hand turn into Station Road. I stopped to look in the window of Stephenson, the chemist. Nowadays, this shop is known as *J Park*. I recently spoke to Mrs Park who told me that the chemist's shop had originally been established in 1917 on the site now occupied by Harpenden Building Society. It transferred to its present location in the 1920s. Mrs Park has run the shop alone since the death of her husband some twenty years ago.

Further down Station Road, I passed another chemist – Clark's (now *Topkins*) until I reached the Midland Bank at the corner with Lower High Street. Which way should I go now? The Common to the left looked inviting enough – a brilliant rain-soaked green, but it was now September. Blackberries and grasses had grown tall, the dark spots of gorse bushes dotted with gold were prolific. There might be gypsies lurking there.

I decided to turn right along the Lower High Street. This looked a picture with the old horse-chestnut tree opposite Thorn, the tobacconist, in full leaf and the gnarled, aged elms lining the greens. I passed several interesting shops and their modern names are given in brackets.

First came Thorn, the tobacconist, where Mr Thorn was actively serving customers, weighing out loose shag tobacco on his fine scales. Outside, a large thermometer, perhaps three feet high, was fixed to the wall.

Next to Thorn's was Harriden's Stores (now *Perry, florist*). This was a high-class grocery with a double-fronted shop window. In one window there was a coffee-roasting machine from which sparks emitted while the roasting of the beans was in progress. The smell was divine.

Then came Dunkley, the butcher (now *Threads*). I remember the sawdust on the floor and the little pay kiosk where the customer paid for her purchases. The butchers never handled cash; they merely cut, weighed and wrapped your order.

Next to Dunkley's was the double-fronted shop called The Forest Stores. This was a large, general store which sold hardware on the left-hand side and groceries on the right. The manager was a bald-headed middle-aged man of rather slight build and wearing a black apron. A pair of pince-nez spectacles adorned his nose. (Nowadays, the premises are the site of *"The Slug and Lettuce" public house*, which incorporates outside coffee tables. The building was re-built some thirty years ago).

Finally, before I reached Vaughan Road, there were two more shops: first, I passed The Empire Meat Company, another butcher (in later years to become *Dewhurst* and, more recently, a *charity shop*). Set back a little from The Empire Meat Company was Bunty's, which in those days also incorporated the premises now

Loading the Groceries

The young shop assistant at Harriden's stores helps the van driver load up in readiness for his delivery round to the large houses in Harpenden. Parking in lower High Street was obviously much easier in the 1930s.

occupied by *Read's*, the florist, and another charity shop. Bunty's went right round the corner of Vaughan Road to include the bread shop now used by *Prudens*. This shop always gave me pleasure. My mother used to take me in to buy Kunzle cakes – some of my favourites – and occasionally we would go upstairs to the café where a jolly good afternoon tea could be had for two shillings (10p).

This, then, was the composition of the shops between Station Road and Vaughan Road on my morning walk that day in September 1933:

1933

MIDLAND BANK / THORN / HARRIDEN's / DUNKLEY / FOREST / EMPIRE / BUNTY's
with offices above   STORES   MEAT
of R G Taylor (Solicitor)   CO.

2003

HSBC BANK / THORN / PERRY / THREADS / SLUG / CHARITY READ's / PRUDEN'S
                                      &   offices
                                  LETTUCE   above

Crossing over Vaughan Road to Pellants, the jewellers and wireless shop, which was on the corner, I looked up to the large electric clock. I couldn't tell the time. I hadn't learned how to. (The face of the clock is still there but without any hands, and the shop is now *Hallmark Cards*). There was little traffic. A few shoppers carrying wicker shopping baskets, and one or two people on bicycles.

I continued walking along the Lower High Street, past the newly-built Methodist Church and the old Brewery House. A high wall kept the brewery private from onlookers in the High Street. Passing the Brewery House (sited where the shop recently vacated by C & A was located), I came to the entrance to the covered market which is now occupied by *Sainsbury's*.

Where the *Abbey National Building Society* now stands, there was a café called "The Swallow" where you could get inexpensive scones and coffee in the morning and tea and cakes in the afternoon – either downstairs or upstairs.

Next to "The Swallow" stood Perry's, florist and greengrocer. Here you could buy a pound of apples for 6d (2½p) even out of the season, as I did a couple of years later as an April birthday present for my mother. The apples were imported from South Africa and, of course, this was before the days of freezing fruit to preserve it.

The covered market was set back (as is *Sainsbury's* today) and a little way along the projection – roughly where *Abbey National's* hole in the wall cash dispenser is sited – you could see "San Toy", a little basement shop which had access via some steps down to the front door. Miss Cooke sold home-made jams, marmalades, lemon curd, honey and many kinds of preserves, and also sweets. She was elderly, with grey hair in a bun and, so it seemed to me, without much sense of humour. She lived on the premises. She had named her tiny shop after a little-known musical comedy which came out in the 1920s.

Looking back, it is difficult to understand how she could have made much profit from such an establishment but I doubt whether she had any kind of mortgage on her home and shop. Most of her produce was home-made which must have kept costs down to a minimum.

Many years later, the shop moved across the High Street to 3, Church Green, the corner now occupied by part of *Connell's*. It retained its name and many years after Miss Cooke's death, continued to be run as a sweet shop.

I will not weary the reader with details of all the shops en route during that morning walk in 1933, but I crossed over eventually opposite Kirkdale Road. I looked at Kirkwick House, the large home of Mr Willis (later to become the Kirkwick Hotel (now the *Gleneagles or Hanover Hotel*) and walked back in the direction of the Common, passing "Florence", the little café with just three tables on the ground floor (now part of *Jacksons*); Jos E West, the baker (with a café upstairs) and a second branch (where *Ashton's* the estate agents are now situated).

There have been many changes to the High Street since those days but it seems that despite the then small population of Harpenden, we were much better served for grocers, small individual shops, and inexpensive cafés.

A plethora of grocers existed quite apart from The Forest Stores and Harriden's. Along the Lower High Street, there was the "Home & Colonial Stores" (*now John Curtis / Halifax plc*); Bentley's (*Lane Fox, estate agents*); and another branch of Bentley's run by Roy Bentley in Station Road. Later in the 1930s, my father's building firm built the "International Stores" which has now become *Nationwide Anglia Building Society*.

Really, in the early 1930s and even after the war, Harpenden was served with as many grocers' shops as it has building societies today.

The main Bentley's Store at 66–68, High Street, was run by Mr Bentley with his eldest son, Edward and youngest son, Don. The old man had an acute business sense. When serving a customer, he used to say, "Mrs Webster, would your little boy like to try one of these biscuits?" This question would be accompanied by a beaming smile wreathed in his moon-like face. He would then open one of the many tins which stored loose biscuits. The biscuit tins lined the wall just as you entered the shop. The child would accept one and show approval. Consequently, the customer would feel duty-bound to buy half a pound.

Harpenden was also well served by bakers, milk suppliers, butchers and greengrocers. I well recall them:

Bakers Jos E West (two branches in the High Street with café on the upper floor).

Rowes (where *Boswell* sandwich bar is now situated at 62, High Street).

Ackroyd's at 36, Station Road (*now a Kebab Shop*).

Milk Harpenden Dairies, Station Road (*now occupied by part of Post Office*).

Waller Dairies, "Bowling Alley" area of Southdown

(Queen's Rd).

Lea Valley Dairies at 12 Leyton Road. (*now occupied by H Smith, Opticians*)

Butchers Dunkley at 7. High Street (*now Threads Giftshop*).

Steabben at the corner of Rothamsted Avenue and Church Green.

Piggott (later Robertson Bros) 32, High Street (*now Challis dress shop*).

Simons at 92, High Street (*now occupied by Jacksons*)

Empire Meat Co. (*later to become Dewhurst*) at 11, High Street.

T H Ganderton at 97, Luton Road.

B Harbour at 115, Southdown Road.

Baxters at 5, Station Road.

Greengrocers J Stanley at 100, High Street (*now Blockbuster Videos*).

C T Jeffs at 2, Bowers Parade.

C T Jeffs at 99, Luton Road.

Fells & Sons at 8, Station Road.

Perry (*now part of Abbey National Building Society*).

O'Dell at 4, Station Road (*later Norbury. Recently converted as an extension to the HSBC Midland Bank*).

It is of continual dismay that so many of these smaller business have now been replaced by three supermarkets, and many shops have sold out their premises to Estate Agents or Building Societies.

On that first day of school in September 1933, I really do not know for how long I walked in the village. I think I asked the time once, but had to have a guess at it later. Eventually, I went back and stood outside Victoria Road School in case it was lunch time and my mother had arrived.

I waited a long time until at last she came. "Hello, you're out already?" she asked. "I thought I was early. How did you get on?"

My deceit did not last long and I admitted that I hadn't been to school. We went home to lunch because no school dinners were available then. In the afternoon, I was taken right into the building to meet my teacher, Miss Jolly, and I was escorted for the rest of the week, sometimes by my mother and sometimes by Ted Mardell, an older boy who lived next door-but-one at Number 28. It would be another week before I was allowed to go to school by myself.

School terrified me. I was frightened of the Headmaster, Mr Watts ('Daddy' Watts) and by the senior teacher, Miss Davis, a forbidding elderly spinster whose white hair was drawn back in a severe bun. She had a sharp tongue and stood no nonsense from anyone.

The only teacher who treated me kindly, and with whom I had any rapport, was Miss Jolly. Sadly, many years later I learned that she had committed suicide.

Victoria Road School was a mixed school for children, known in those days as an 'elementary' school. Teaching was virtually confined to the three 'Rs' with a little art work in between, but not nearly as much of the latter as you find in today's primary schools.

At break time, morning and afternoon, you were sent out into the playground where you fended for yourself. The playground (which is today occupied by the library building) was tarmac-surfaced and surrounded by tall, iron railings, presumably to prohibit escape. There were no organised games or P.E. offered by the teachers. In fact, they were nowhere to be seen. Consequently, any bullying by the larger boys went undetected. 'Gangs' were prevalent and until you were invited to join a 'gang', you were not really accepted, and were left virtually friendless. The invitation to join was accomplished by the leader at the head of a piece of rope about twelve feet long, followed by his cronies each holding their part of the rope, asking you to get on the end. After that you were a member of his gang and at every playtime, each member had to take up his position strictly according to this position of seniority – the leader at the front, right down to the newest member at the end. Woe betide anyone who positioned himself in the wrong order. It sounds ridiculous now but I remember a good half-dozen of these rope-gangs parading round the playground, each rope having between eight and twelve children holding it.

So my education at Victoria Road School continued.

Every lunch time, I would walk home to Willoughby Road and then back again to school, often accompanied by friends dropped off or picked up en route. This would be repeated at the end of school in the late afternoon.

There was so little traffic that only a cursory glance was needed when crossing Carlton Road. I remember breaking up for the Christmas holiday and running across Carlton Road opposite Carlton Bank, trailing behind me a long paper chain of Christmas link-chain decorations a good twenty feet in length – the result of considerable time spent during the art-work sessions of term time.

I always looked forward to Christmastide. I enjoyed the frost and making slides in the playground, when it was cold enough and the ice sufficiently thick. My friends and I delighted in making slides on the ponds on the Common. Again, the gang situation crept in. Having made your slide, you and your friends would never allow another gang to share it. (How the weaknesses of human nature show themselves at such an early age.)

Above all, at Christmas time I enjoyed Anscombe's shop. This was an old-fashioned store – a mini Selfridges – which became the centre piece of Harpenden's shopping in the 1930s. Situated in Leyton Road on the site now occupied by *Waitrose*, its basement was converted around the second week in December into a Father Christmas's Grotto. To entice you in and down the stairs to the basement, there was normally an elaborate electric train set, fully working, displayed in the window at street level, on the right hand of the shop's northern entrance.

There were three main entrances: one to the south near to the owner's private house (Wellington House) which led into the gloves, laces, stockings, haberdashery and costume jewellery departments; one in the centre which was the most grandiose, leading to the central hall and the men's department; and, finally, the entrance to the north which led into the furnishings department.

By each counter, provided in each section of the store, could

Anscombe Stores c.1930

Harpenden's own Emporium of Commerce. It boasted of selling everything from a suite of furniture to a reel of cotton. The old elm trees can be seen on the right hand side of the picture.

Anscombe Stores c.1900

Anscombe Stores c.1960
A more modern look to the store, (and to Leyton Road itself). The old elms
had long gone, and were situated where the parked car can be seen. The
Regent Cinema (right) was used by Anscombes in the 1960s as a furniture
department.

be found two high, old-fashioned, round, wooden chairs, the kind
with cane seats. This was to enable a lady to be seated whilst
giving her order or waiting to be served.

The shop contained a sedate array of brass fittings, glass-
fronted fixtures framed in natural oak and solid mahogany sales
counters which had been carefully polished and lovingly
preserved over the years. In the centre of the store on the ground
floor, there was a cash desk to which overhead wires transported

the bills and receipts by means of metal carriers and detachable wooden cups which were catapulted to and from the counters. This was called the "Lamson Rapid-wire Overhead Transport System" and was installed originally in 1852. It was still in perfect working order when the store finally closed in 1982. It thus served Anscombe's for 130 years!

Anscombe's Store was originally opened in 1848 and boasted of selling everything from a suite of furniture to a reel of Coates cotton. Indeed, you could purchase buttons, ribbons, cottons, fancy handkerchiefs, personal leather luggage, pinafores, shopping bags, bed linen, towels, men's wear, and so on. It was a kind of Gamages or Selfridges for the people of Harpenden.

The precise date is not known of Wellington House, which remained the home of the successive owners of Anscombe's throughout their generations. It is earlier than its name might suggest. The first reference to the house comes in a mortgage to Mrs Martha Large in 1759. Ten years later, it was known as Mr Cole's house and in 1785 it was bought by a Mrs Legh whose relative, Henrietta Maria Townley Balfour, made a 'camera obscura' sketch of the house in about 1800. After Anscombe's shop was demolished in the mid-1980s to make way for the Waitrose store, this sketch was discovered in Dublin and now takes pride of place on the first floor landing of Wellington House which is occupied by Aldwyck Housing Association Limited.

Wellington House, presumably so named in about 1815 in honour of the Iron Duke and his victories, was bought by Mr A Anscombe in 1869 for £670.00. The house had a combined use as shop, office, and living accommodation for the family and also for the 'living in' assistants. In 1880, the Leyton Road side was built into a shop extension but unfortunately this completely destroyed the original eastern elevation of the house.

In 1962 Mr Algernon Pamphilon became the Managing Director of Anscombe's which was later owned by Mr Pamphilon and a consortium of directors. Later, in the late 1940s, Algy Pamphilon's sons, Bryan and Dennis, joined the firm and ran Anscombe's after their father's death, until it was sold to the John Lewis Partnership in 1982 for the establishment of Waitrose.

Their mother, Violet (Vi), also a director, could always be seen in the central cash desk, amid the almost constant sound of humming and swishing as the wooden cups containing customers' cash and bills of sale sped on their way to the cubicle. Here, their arrival was signalled by a succession of metallic clunks as each carrier docked in its station. Vi would check the contents and by the time the customer's purchase had been neatly parcelled up, the singing of the wires would herald the speedy approach of the returning carrier, complete with change and receipt.

During the 1940s, I became a frequent visitor to Wellington House to listen to Bryan Pamphilon playing the white grand piano in the front room or his pianola which stood in the hall. The pianola was fascinating; it was operated by the pedals and the piano rolls depressed the keys as though someone were actually playing. The Pamphilons had some rare, early jazz piano rolls which played 'ragtime' after the style of Scott Joplin. I've often wondered whether they were in fact original Scott Joplin rolls, made from the actual playing of the composer himself.

Christmastide was the time for looking into shop windows. There were always mouth-watering displays in Harriden's and Bentley's. York hams, Stilton cheeses, crackers, snowmen, cakes and Christmas puddings filled their windows from the beginning of December onwards.

I remember being taken by my parents to a Christmas pantomime in 1933 and walking home to Willoughby Road. When we got as far as Lea Road, the frost sparkled on the red paving slabs of the footpath which glistened all the way down. The pantomime had been performed in the old Church Hall in Amenbury Lane which, today, is the offices of a financial company. I do not recall any details of the pantomime but I do remember those paving slabs which made up the footpath in Lea Road. I recently re-visited Lea Road and ascertained that the red slabs were still there, some 70 years later – a marvellous tribute to the quality of the materials used in those days.

Willoughby Road is a good mile from Victoria Road, and this meant that I had to walk at least four miles every day on my journeys to and from school, including the lunch break. I normally looked forward to the afternoon journey back to school because I had either a halfpenny or penny to spend on sweets in the shop now occupied by the kebab shop in Station Road. If I didn't have any money, I used to beg a penny from anyone I knew. Sometimes, I used to see Mr Mann returning to work after his lunch break. He was the factory manager of Abbott, Anderson and Abbott, and a friend of my father. Abbott, Anderson and Abbott manufactured waterproof clothing in a large factory sited on the location of Harpenden's new fire station in Leyton Road. I am ashamed to say that I frequently asked, "Could you please spare a penny, Mr Mann?" He never refused. The sweet shop was a favourite with the school children, being en route so to speak. It sold sweets for as little as a farthing each, so I could get four for a penny.

Inevitably, one day I was entrusted by my mother to do an errand for her while she looked after my small brother at home. I had to collect something from Stephenson's, the chemist in Station Road. This was to be done at lunch-time when I could bring the purchase straight home. I was given half-a-crown. Although this converts to only 12½ pence, I suppose the sum in those days was equivalent to a £5 note in today's purchasing power.

After break-time in the morning, I noticed that the half crown was missing. I looked everywhere I could around the playground before running home at lunch-time to tell my mother the news. You would have thought that a fortune had been lost, equivalent at least to the entire contents of Fort Knox! Both my parents accompanied me back to school and after leaving me to take my place in the classroom, they went to see the Headmaster, Mr Watts (nicknamed 'Daddy' Watts by the children). At 3.00 p.m. I was summoned to the Headmaster's study and I quaked. Nobody was sent to the Headmaster unless some misdemeanour had been committed. I had quite forgotten about the half crown!

Mr Watts, greying gingery coloured hair, looking stern and seated at his desk boomed, "Ralph, I believe you were careless enough to lose a half crown which you had in your possession this morning!"

"Yes, Mr Watts."

"Well, it's been found. Take it back home to your mother and don't lose it again!"

Oh, the relief! Not at the finding of the money which I had lost, but that I had not been accused of doing anything wrong. I have since wondered at the wisdom of entrusting a five-year old child to make a purchase with what was a fair sum of money in the days of 1933.

My life at Victoria Road School continued unremarkably. I went from Miss Jolly's class into the class of Miss Davis, the ogre of whom I was frightened to death. I was never summoned to the Headmaster again, although he used to pass me, pedalling his old-fashioned bicycle along Carlton Road heading back to school after lunch. I tried to be on my best behaviour when I saw him.

I suppose between the ages of 5 and 7½, I had learned very elementary numeracy and to be able to read and write simple things so long as the words were printed. I have sometimes wondered whether the fact that I did not achieve more was the fault of the school, or of me. I am inclined to think the latter. I was not particularly bright!

In those early days, the only thing I ever did to cause my father to be in any way proud of his son, was to win a race on Harpenden Common during the 1935 Silver Jubilee celebrations of King George V. The races for children (and adults too) were held on the part of the Common which is below the cricket pitch. My prize was a small yacht which I sailed happily for many years on the Silver Cup pond just south of the Baa-lamb trees. The race itself was a 50 yards sprint and I was as surprised as anyone that I came first.

The filling in of the Silver Cup pond during the 1970s was, in my view, one of Harpenden's tragedies. A particular Harpenden Urban District Councillor, Dr Miller, persuaded his fellow councillors that the pond was a health hazard and it was filled in. Dr Miller departed to Canada, leaving Harpenden without its

The Silver Cup Pond
Where children spent many a happy hour sailing their boats, but thought to be
a health hazard and filled in. The baa-lamb trees are on the right.

sailing pond. Ernest Ackroyd (of Ackroyd's bakery), one of Harpenden's longest serving members of the Council, promised that Harpenden would get back the Silver Cup pond before he died, but it didn't happen. All that can be seen today is the indentation in the grass near the children's sand pit area.

1935 and the King's Silver Jubilee gave Harpenden the opportunity to show what it could do in its own contribution to the celebrations. What a magnificent contribution that was! The village was converted into a magical place.

The greens between the Lower High Street and the main High Street looked like fairyland. The trees were festooned with

Station Road, Decorated for the 1935 Jubilee
The Midland Bank (now HSBC) can be seen in the left hand foreground, and
Trustrams (newsagents) in the right hand foreground.

bunting tied from one tree to another. Chinese lanterns were
hung in the trees themselves, and small glass jars were suspended
from the chains, which surrounded the greens. Each glass jar was
coloured and contained a wax night light for illumination. All the
greens were treated like this but I particularly remember how
pretty the area looked under the famous horse-chestnut tree on
the Green near the Midland Bank.

Individual shop owners played their part too, draping their
premises with Union Jacks and planting red, white and blue
flowers in planters above the shop fascias.

For a brief time, Harpenden's people forgot their worries,

relaxed and enjoyed the celebrations. They watched a grand parade of floats, Morris dancing, local schools' contributions, and feasted, drank and celebrated the jubilee of their King and Queen.

Prices too were comparatively cheap. An advertisement placed in the 1935 Jubilee brochure by F Timson of 57, High Street, offered Rubber-Soled Gentlemen's shoes for 10/6d per pair (52½p). Mr Timson was a boot-maker and repairer when he started his business in the early part of this century, and expanded it to become a general outfitter. The same brochure offered Gents' Flannel Trousers from 4/6d (22½p) to 14/6d (72½p).

CHAPTER FOUR

The Move to Bowers House

In 1936, my father bought Bowers House for £800. It all began with a Green-Line bus.

My father had recently dissolved his partnership with Mr Harvey who wanted to retire, and he had decided to set up his own business. Thus, the firm of H E Webster Limited (Building Contractors) was founded. Although the builders' yard in Willoughby Road and the small office in Kirkdale Road were retained, he wanted somewhere with an address in the High Street which could be used as an office and with a small yard. Bowers House then came on the market and my father saw that both these criteria could be accomplished, together with a move to an upmarket, private residence. So he decided to move from Willoughby Road.

Prior to this, the previous resident had been Dr W H Blake who had lived and practised there from 1892 until his death in 1933. Even to this day, you can see the old bracket which held the gas lamp outside his surgery at the northern end of the house. Dr Blake achieved some small notoriety inasmuch as he became the first person in England to be knocked down and killed by a Green-Line bus. The Green-Lines were single-decker coaches which provided a half-hourly service between Luton and Guildford (via Harpenden, St Albans, Barnet, and Oxford Street in London).

Dr Blake was a bachelor and had no immediate relatives. Consequently, his Estate was divided amongst those distant relatives who could be traced, and it was handled, I believe, by Mr Ronald G Taylor (solicitor) who was also a member of Harpenden Urban District Council. The Estate Agent who handled the sale of Bowers House was Mr Leslie Gillow of Gillow, Brading and Elm

Time for Tea

Dignitaries standing in front of Bowers House after the unveiling of the war memorial across the High Street, 9th October 1920. They were entertained to tea by Dr.Blake. Lieut-General Lord Cavan (ADC to King George V) performed the unveiling. He lived in Wheathampstead, and can be seen in uniform in the centre of the picture.

Bowers House Before 1936
The lawns swept down to the Lower High Street.

(now re-named Brading and Harmer) who was also a member of the Council. A third person involved was Mr C F Putterill, timber merchant (and also a member of the Council) whose garden backed onto the Bowers House grounds.

Between them, the grounds of Bowers House were carved up. The back land was sold to Mr Putterill and the frontage sold for the development of Bowers Parade. My father bought the remainder.

Presumably, permission for the development of Bowers Parade was granted by the then Surveyor to Harpenden U.D.C., Mr Johnson, but in those days it was not necessary to obtain separate planning permission as we do today. (This did not become

Bowers House Today, Hidden from View

mandatory until the Planning Act of 1947 came into force).

If the people of Harpenden were not worried about the development of Bowers Parade in 1936, they should begin to contemplate it now. The wonderful architecture of Bowers House became completely hidden from view. If only it were not unrealistic to consider demolishing this typical 1930s parade of shops and restore to view the glories of Bowers House!

My father retained a small private garden but used most of the remaining grounds for a builder's yard, served by a narrow access road from the Lower High Street. He erected a joinery shop in the northern part of the grounds (opposite Dr Blake's erstwhile surgery) which was later to be used as The Salvation Army Forces'

The Southern End of Bowers House Today
(*Now converted into a maisonette*) Showing the southern side of Bowers
Parade on the left hand side of the picture.

Canteen during the 1939–45 War.

He sold off a portion at the southern end of the house as a maisonette but retained a couple of ground floor rooms, which he used as offices. He also converted a portion of the northern wing into two flats (a ground floor flat and a first floor flat), retaining the remaining centre portion of Bowers House as our residence.

I well remember being taken round the house for the first time. This was just before my eighth birthday. Never before had I been in such a large house. It seemed enormous! This, of course, was before part of the house had been converted into flats and was the

Bowers House, circa 1900

A swan kennel can be seen on the left hand side. This provided shelter for the pair of swans which used to swim on the pond. The latter has long since been filled in, but was located to the left of The Cross Keys public house.

original whole residence in which Dr Blake had lived. My father, I recall, was talking to the Estate Agent and I soon became bored with their conversation. After a while, I slipped away to explore this huge house by myself. First, up the staircase then quickly along the first floor corridors as far as I could go. At the end, I found a steep staircase, which led to the second floor. All was well until I attempted the return trip and I realised that I was lost. I must have taken a wrong turning somewhere. Fancy getting lost in a house! I had to call out to my father who, hearing the direction of my voice, came to my rescue.

The entrance hall to the house gave an impression of grandeur. The floor is tiled here whilst the rest of the house is floored with wide oak boards. The main entrance hall door is made of solid oak, two inches thick. Originally, it was made completely of wood, the windows having been added at a later date.

The living-room of this part of Bowers House has a handsome brick and wood fireplace which almost certainly dates from the earliest times. The mantelpiece is one huge piece of timber, only roughly shaped to fit. My parents had an Indian carpet laid in this room. If I rolled on it, the long hairs adhered to my clothes. The piano was also put into the living-room and I remember trying to play the tunes of the day.

Another ground floor room – on the right of the main entrance hall having entered by the main entrance door – we used as our dining-room. At that time, it was completely panelled in oak. The panelling was in superb condition and included two hidden doors, difficult to detect. Both were blocked off. One originally had led into the room which my father converted into an office, and the other into the southern end of the house, which had been sold off as a maisonette. Regrettably, the panelling was sold to an American for £1,000 in the 1960s and transported across the Atlantic to the U.S.A. The open fireplace in the dining-room had a beautiful over mantel with carved panels which reached almost to the ceiling.

The main staircase was built in this new part of the house and although it is not known exactly when it was done, it was probably in the 17th century. It is of circular design with a large 'well' so that when mounting its gentle flight, you can almost see the tiled floor below. I remember when my parents visited the

The Dining Room at Bowers House
With its original oak panelling (later sold and shipped to America). The wrought
iron fire grate contained two brass finials shaped like Victorian champagne
glasses and which needed frequent polishing.

Paris Exhibition of 1936, they brought back a toy parachutist whose 'chute opened from the pack on his back when dropped from a height or tossed up into the air. I spent many happy hours dropping him over the staircase well from the landing above and watching the parachute float downwards to the hall below.

Halfway up the main staircase, there is a small door, which gives the impression of being a cupboard. However, when the door is opened, it reveals a narrow, steep staircase, which leads to a small, chilly room on the second floor. I think it must have once been used as a maid's room but I remember – even as a child – how eerie this secondary staircase and room felt. I am not superstitious but the evil aura which this room gave out was the nearest I have ever felt to being amongst the supernatural. About ten years ago, I re-visited Bowers House and the chill and unease in this room are still present.

The house abounds with beams and vertical timbers of all shapes and sizes; some of the larger of which could well have come from ships judging by their bowed shape and the man-made holes in them.

The cellar is very small and not at all in keeping with the size and age of the remainder of the house. The arch in one wall has been bricked up and it is almost certain that the rest of the cellar is still there. There is said to be a secret passage leading from the house to St Nicholas's Church. It caved in years ago, so the owner at that time had the entrance (which was in the cellar) permanently blocked up.

The corridor on the first floor has oak beams in its ceiling and walls. It is floored with wide oak boards and the bedrooms lead off from this corridor. Half way along, there is a very large bedroom with a high ceiling and a huge Elizabethan fireplace made of solid stone. On one of the window panes the name 'Polly Stirling' has been scratched onto the glass with a diamond. There is no date, but the 'S' is similar to a modern 'f" and this style of writing was prevalent in the seventeenth and eighteenth centuries. We used this room as a sports room, complete with snooker table and boxing punch ball which my father installed.

It is not certain how Bowers House got its name. However, the name Bower does appear in the history of the Harpenden area some time after 1391 when sixty acres of land known as

Cotersend passed into the hands of a Roger Bower. The name Cotersend, or Cootersend, as it is known today, still exists. It is the name of a farm north of Harpenden. It is likely that Roger Bower lived at some time in Harpenden and gave his name to his residence – Bowers House.

The first person who left written confirmation of having lived in Bowers House was Richard Bardolf, the fourth son of Edmund Bardolf of Rothamsted. He was there during the sixteenth and early seventeenth centuries. His will, leaving his house "called Bowers" to his son, Richard, is one of the earliest documents referring to the property. The will and the inventory of goods and 'chattels' which accompanied it, make fascinating reading:

"In a roome over the Stayres Heads", for example, were to be found "the several lumber there", carpets, plate, brass, pewter, "linnen" of all sorts. "The apparell of the testator (Richard Bardolf) and his wives' apparel", wood, "fruite, poultrie" and of all things "the compost", all of which were worth the princely sum of £27.11s.4d. Probably the "roome over the Stayres Heads" referred to the chilly room which I found so eerie and to which access was gained by the little staircase half-way up the main staircase.

The estate was later sold to Sir John Wittewronge and became part of the Rothamsted Estate, to which it belonged until the beginning of the twentieth century when Dr Blake lived in the house and practised medicine there. Sir John Wittewronge's portrait still hangs in Rothamsted Manor.

Many people were tenants of the house, including rectors of the parish nobility, and doctors. In 1810, the Reverend G D Knox married Miss Marrianne Shearman and they lived at Bowers House until his death in 1812. The widow then married John

Bennet Lawes of Rothamsted, and became the mother of Sir John Bennet Lawes, the famous agricultural scientist whose research led to great changes in agriculture throughout the world.

With the move to Bowers House came a new school for me – Moreton End. I think that my father was reasonably satisfied with the financial arrangements which evolved from the dissolution of his partnership with Mr Harvey and, with his newly-found wealth and status of owning his company, he decided that with his more up-market house should go a more up-market school for me. So came my first day – my mother having 'kitted' me out with the school uniform, sports gear, etc. – I presented myself to have my speech criticised, but also to find new friends.

CHAPTER FIVE

Life at Moreton End School

As was the case with my previous school in Victoria Road, I was afraid of the Headmaster. Mr V E H Card, having opened the school and become its first Headmaster in 1933, had had three years to settle Moreton End into a well-run "ship", and its daily routine ran like well-oiled clockwork. The number of pupils had increased from five to thirty-four. Mr Card was a strict disciplinarian, acquired no doubt when he worked as a Maths teacher at Hardenwick School, under the headship of Mr H B Evington, scholar of Marlborough and Magdalene College, Cambridge.

"Hard-boiled Egg" – as the boys at Hardenwick School had extended Mr Evington's initials – had been in the Indian Army during the early part of the twentieth century and had brought much of the discipline of army life – later to rub off on Mr Card – to Hardenwick School. Hardenwick occupied almost the whole of Wordsworth Road on the west side, whilst many of the school houses occupied much of its eastern side.

It is interesting to note that H B Evington, whilst out in India, became friendly with Humphrey Grose-Hodge, who was himself destined to become Headmaster of Bedford School in the 1930s and '40s. There was much similarity between the two men: both were of small stature but able, by means of a mere look, to command instant silence; both enjoyed a great deal of respect from the boys and their parents alike.

Many older Harpenden residents may also recall H B Evington riding his old-fashioned upright bicycle in Harpenden, trailing a huge St Bernard dog (Ben) on a lead, which meant, of course, that he rarely had proper control of his cycle. The bike had originally been designed for a lady because of the curved cross bar and it still contained the string guards to the rear wheel which would have prevented a lady's skirts from getting caught up in it. I remember many occasions when he came to grief and a helpful passer-by would be obliged to help him up and untangle the dog's lead from the spokes.

If he went to collect his daily newspaper from Whitehouse Newsagents (*now Balfour*), he would prop up his bicycle on the kerb outside the shop and tie his dog's lead to it. Of course, a St Bernard is a very powerful dog and it only seemed a moment after H.B.E. had entered the shop when the dog would pull the bicycle over. I had a few friends at Hardenwick School who used to regale stories of how they were sometimes blamed for a wet 'puddle' on the floor of their classroom, when the real culprit was Ben.

In my first year at Moreton End School, I did not have much contact with Mr Card except for the odd Maths lesson. He seemed to concentrate more on the older boys. I did come into contact with him, however, if I stayed to school lunch. I hated this because I was not a lover of meat and in pre-war days to have vegetarian inclinations was simply unfashionable, if not strange. It was considered 'unmanly' not to eat meat. Consequently, there was no question of being allowed to leave any on the plate. I remember on one occasion, Mr Card stood over me whilst I tried to swallow a thick lump of fat which had been served up. It nearly made me sick! Normally, I walked home to lunch at Bowers House but if the weather was inclement, my mother would ring up the school and ask if I could stay to lunch. This 'extra' would then go onto the term's bill. I used to look out of the classroom window with some anxiety from about 11.00 a.m. onwards in case it looked like rain, which would prompt my mother to telephone, and leave me saddled with a school lunch which I dreaded.

I used to enjoy my walk back to school after lunch at about 1.15 p.m. The threat of a school lunch had disappeared at least for another twenty-four hours, and afternoons were normally filled with sport or by an interesting lecture if the weather was bad: never lessons in the afternoon.

So, I used to leave the lunch table at Bowers House with a light heart, and make my way back to Moreton End School. First, I would pass the new shops in Bowers Parade and the newly-opened showrooms of Reads Motor Works. Here were displayed the latest 1936 models of Austin, Morris, and B.S.A. cars, each of which could be acquired for a few hundred pounds.

After passing the Forester's Arms public house (recently *Threshers*), I came to Lines, the blacksmiths. I always paused here for a few minutes to watch Mr Lines shoe a horse or pump up the fire with the bellows. Sometimes, his assistant would do the shoeing, and I still remember the smell as the red hot metal shoe was applied to the horse's hoof and hammered to ensure a good fit.

Lower High Street
This picture was taken where Anvil Parade and Threshers off-Licence premises
are located today. The ancient elms were later removed as part of a road
improvement scheme.

The premises of Lines Blacksmiths were demolished at the end of
the 1950s to make way for a new parade of shops with flats over
them, aptly named "Anvil House".

The Lines family name goes back in Harpenden's history to the
1600s, and they were involved during the nineteenth century in
the building and administration of the old Congregational church
in Vaughan Road, which later merged with the United Reformed
movement.

Towards the end of the nineteenth century, old Henry Lines
would shoe the horses at the Harpenden race-course on the

Common, and later fashioned and forged Westfield Cemetery's huge wrought-iron gates. The last surviving male member of the Lines family died in February 1991, and only daughters survived, one still living at the family house in Southdown Road.

Next, I came to 57 High Street. This house (now occupied as a restaurant) was divided into two shops – T Chambers, Hairdresser, and F Timson, Shoe and Boot-maker. Upstairs, Frank Bentley had an office for his painting and decorating business and a large sign outside on the first floor advertised it.

Old Tom Chambers, with nicotine-stained moustache, continually coughed and wheezed. You could hear this from the outside pavement as you passed by. He never seemed to stop clearing his phlegm, even when cutting someone's hair. Tom was always busy, no doubt due to the fact that his prices were cheap. Sixpence (2½ pence) for a short back and sides, and many a schoolboy, sent there by his mother, emerged with a 'pudding basin' style, more suitable to the Army. Strangely, Tom also carried out repairs to umbrellas and there was always a stack inside the hairdressing shop, awaiting attention or collection. Old Tom was kept so busy that eventually he had to employ an assistant, Mr Simpson, nicknamed 'Professor' because of his apparent ability to talk about any subject. Anyone requiring a slightly more up-market haircut went to S.W. Gaskin in Leyton Road (now *Snips*) where a good cut, complete with dressing, etc. could be had for one shilling (5p).

In the other half of the building, which had been converted into a shop, F. Timson carried out his business of selling boots and shoes. He had made progress since earlier in the century when his occupation had been almost totally boot-making in the tiniest of detached shops sited at the end of the footpath which runs past Taylor Walker's offices at 65, High Street. I believe that originally this small building was used as the Tolls office from which the name of "Tollgate House" was later given to the home of Captain Guy Lydekker's family at 65–69, High Street, although up to the end of the 1939/45 war it was known as "The White House". This footpath was heavily lined with aged elms which gave shade to the front of The White House. Later, just after the war, this house was to be opened as The Tollgate Hotel, but nowadays has been converted into offices and shops.

At the end of The White House and on the corner of Sun Lane was the old half-timbered Sun Lane Cottage. This was formerly called "Harvest House" and was much bigger than it is today, now occupied by an estate agent. Part was demolished when Sun Lane was widened. The old elms have also long since gone, to be replaced by raised flower beds.

Instead of going along the Tollgate footpath, I would cross over to the other side of the main road at this point. This would bring me outside Hubert Thurston, the photographer. The business had been started by his father, Frederick Thurston, who had photographed members of the Royal Family, including Queen Mary and the Princesses Elizabeth and Margaret. The quality, expression and character of the sitter in Mr Thurston's black and white portraits (taken with an old-fashioned plate camera and tripod) far exceeded the clarity of today's coloured photographs.

Next to Thurston's, there was Read's Motors with petrol pumps situated on the pavement to enable cars to fill up whilst parked at the road kerbside. This was the 'working' department of Read's Motors who retained the double-fronted showrooms in Bowers

Reads Showrooms in 1939
Located at the northern end of Bowers Parade, some of whose shops were
not yet 'let'. On the left hand side of the picture can be seen 'The Foresters
Arms', later to become Threshers.

Parade solely for display. Outside, Charlie Read, portly and normally wearing a trilby hat, would be seen chatting to customers. His role was purely public relations with the patrons. All day he spent talking to people and, very occasionally, he would fill the petrol tank of a favoured customer. Inside, behind the scenes, his brother, Bill, slight and slim, sporting a workman's flat cap, would be up to his elbows in grease, unseen by the public. He was the engineer and mechanic in the business. Years later, the premises were demolished and rebuilt. The old building was mainly of wood and glass construction with no 'pull-in' for cars, but the new premises, of brick construction, were set further back with a driveway in front, enabling Read's Motors to continue trading as a garage. Today, the premises are occupied by the tyre and exhaust company '*Kwik Fit*'.

A little further along, I used to pass Putterill's Garage (the site now occupied by *C. Wilson, plant hire*). This garage also had its pumps on the pavement. This was normal in the 1930s. The garage was owned by the brother of the timber merchant in Thompson's Close, and specialised in Rover and Singer cars.

Having crossed Kirkdale Road, I would pass the former home of Mr Willis, which had been converted into "The Kirkdale Hotel" but still retained the confines of the original house. It would be many years before extensions took place and the hotel was renamed "The Gleneagle". (Recently, the hotel changed its name yet again and is currently "*The Hanover International Hotel*").

After crossing Townsend Lane, I passed "Caravans", a company which was owned by Major Arnold Foster. A caravan was displayed on the roof of the premises. I often wondered how it had got up there. After the war, Colonel Walker joined the company and it amused me that the junior partner held more senior military rank.

Behind the caravan company in Townsend Lane was the home of Leslie Burgin, Member of Parliament for Luton. The large house known as "Aplins" stood in extensive grounds hidden by a tall hedge, but the house and grounds fell into the hands of developers in the 1970s and the Aplins Close development took place.

In the 1930s, the old-established motor garage "Oggelsby's" was to be found only in Southdown Road (recently *South Harpenden Cars* occupied the premises). It would be some years before Oggelsby's would be established in Luton Road. Then, on the site of the present Oggelsby's petrol filling station, stood the "Austral Cinema", later to be re-named "The Embassy" before its eventual demise around 1980.

The Austral was owned by Captain Webb who lived opposite in the house called "The Doon". Captain Webb had spent many years in Australia, hence the name given to the cinema which was managed by a very live wire, Mr Buckman, who used to dress up and appear on the cinema's stage to advertise such films as "The Phantom of the Opera" or "The Hunchback of Notre Dame", which really encouraged him to indulge in a bit of play-acting during the interval.

My father's firm had been given the job of providing the advertising panels which adorned each side of the main entrance at the upper floor level, and he sub-let the work to a local sign-writer, Bob Spencer. Bob was not only a sign-writer but also a fairly capable artist. He was of slight build, wore a flat cap, was articulate and had a high intelligence. I don't think he ever made a great deal of money from his profession, despite his obvious talents. His task was to paint a kangaroo on the left-hand panel and an emu on the right – both symbols representing Australia. I well remember a furious argument developing between my father at ground level and Bob on his step ladder at upper level, concerning the emu and how it should look. Because of the distance between, the argument rose in decibels to a shouting match which culminated in Bob Spencer taking up his step ladders, packing up his paints and brushes, hoisting the ladders over his shoulders and cycling back to his home on Crossway (there being no motorised transport available to manual workers). After a couple of days, my father called round at his house to resolve the argument somehow. I expect he apologised, and Bob went back to complete the picture of the emu on the advertising panel.

On my way back to school, I used to feel very envious of the ladies, normally middle-aged, who were forming a short queue to get into the Austral cinema before the afternoon's performance. The doors opened at 1.30 p.m. in readiness for the programme which commenced at 2.00 p.m. After paying for their ticket at the kiosk, sixpence *(2½p)* downstairs, ninepence *(4p)* upstairs, they would order afternoon tea. This would consist of a tray of tea, passed along during the interval to the person who had ordered it. The cost was 1/6d *(7½p)* and for this you received a pot of tea, bread and butter, jam and a scone or small cake. I used to think to myself, "Lucky devils, going to the cinema whilst I've got to go to school!" However, I continued on my way, hurried past Mr Theodore Schofield's dental practice at the bottom of Douglas Road, and into the school's side gate in Moreton End Lane.

The curriculum for the afternoon was normally sport. Boys changed in the cellar, trying to avoid the huge stalk of green bananas which was suspended from a spike in the ceiling. After getting into our sports 'gear', we would then proceed to walk up Moreton End Lane to the hockey field *(now part of Roundwood School's playing fields)*, a comparatively short walk. Cricket was played in the summer; soccer during the winter term, and athletics practised during the Easter and summer terms. The school owned a small timber hut at the side of the field, which housed some of the more cumbersome items such as the score board, which could not be easily transported from the school every day. Bats were kept well oiled to maintain their good condition and the hut's pervading smell was of linseed oil.

Once, the senior boys tried to build an aeroplane, supervised by Mr Card. It was called "The Flying Flea" – an early Do-It-Yourself effort. All components were finally put together on the playing field, but it never flew!

After the annual Sports Day in the summer, parents and boys returned to the school for the presentation of prizes on the lawn and, afterwards, were invited to take tea provided by Mrs Card.

School continued to a regular pattern. Lessons in the morning preceded by assembly at 9.00 a.m.; lunch 12.30 – 2.00 p.m.; sport in the afternoon. There was morning break at 11.00 a.m. for which we assembled in the front downstairs room. In the winter, we were given a cup of cocoa and one biscuit; in the summer, home-made lemonade, using lemonade crystals, and a banana (from the cellar), or an orange with the top cut off and eaten with a tea-spoon!

Once, in assembly, Mr Card, looking his most serious, announced that one of the mothers – Mrs Jeremy who lived in Kirkdale Road – had telephoned to complain that her son had been punched 'below the belt' during a fight which had taken place in the cellar changing-room the previous afternoon. I searched the faces of my fellow pupils to see if I could read any sign of guilt which would have given away the identity of the miscreant. I could not. Whoever it was, was hiding his guilt extremely well.

"Webster," thundered Mr Card, "Stand out in front!" I was thunderstruck. What had it to do with me? Uneasily, I cast my mind back to the previous afternoon. My recollection was vague although I did recall a playful tiff with Micky Jeremy, but certainly no hard punches had been thrown. I diligently stood out in front. "Webster," repeated Mr Card, "I think you are well aware of the incident to which I refer. Come to my study at break-time."

I visualised that I would be caned for something which I could not remember. Mr Card seemed to enjoy caning. In fact, hardly a day passed without Michael Veitch, the vicar's son, being caned for some misdemeanour. I felt indignant and, when break came, looked cautiously round the door of the Headmaster's study. He was not there! That was enough for me. I had done as bidden and had no intention of presenting myself in his study again. I didn't go back and, for some reason which I was never able to discover, I never heard another word about the matter.

Despite Mr Card's stern discipline, he tried to instil in the boys a sense of fair play and decent behaviour. When Remembrance Day on November 11th came near, poppies were on sale at the school, priced at one penny, sixpence (these included an artificial leaf), and 2/6d (*12½p*) for a very swanky affair suitable for placing at the front of a car. Mr Card always made a point of telling the whole school at Assembly that he had put 2/6d. into the box but had only taken out a one penny poppy for his buttonhole. I never understood the logic of this but I realise he was trying to make a point.

On Boat Race days, we were encouraged to 'sport' either light or dark blue ribbons to indicate whether we supported Cambridge or Oxford. Although these rosettes could be obtained from street vendors in Harpenden, they were on sale at the school and the proceeds were given to one of Mr Card's charities. I supported Cambridge, simply because they normally won!

Moreton End School had quite a good library and the Headmaster encouraged us to have a liking for books and the ability to obtain knowledge from them. The latest "National Geographical Magazine" was always available. Mr Card's aim for us all was to be able to think and obtain a base knowledge of many things. Consequently, particularly on wet afternoons, we had a discussion lesson. Any sort of question could be fired at Mr Card, from flying above the stratosphere to all the topics of the day. Once a boy put up his hand and asked, "Please, sir, is it true that babies come from the doctor's black bag?" Butterflies and moths were frequently discussed and Mr Card kept a very large and interesting collection.

Sometimes, on wet, wintry afternoons, when it really wasn't fit to play soccer, the school would assemble – all except the smallest boys – in the front room downstairs for a lecture by Mr Card, aided by his epidiascope – a kind of overhead projector which would project an object or slide (placed on its horizontal plate) onto the screen. The sheet used for the screen was a linen bed sheet bearing the date 1875. One of the boys, Ian Hurt, had a father who was a keen philatelist, and Mr Hurt once loaned two valuable stamps to show. Unfortunately, Mr Card went on talking, unaware that the heat from the epidiascope was curling up the stamps! I do not think it caused any lasting damage.

Visiting lecturers included a deep-sea diver who dressed up in his complete diving outfit, including his helmet. He brought with him an underwater cutting tool – very up-to-date at that time –

and demonstrated its use by filling a large biscuit tin full of water, then worked from the inside! The resultant flood of water on the floor was a great success with the boys. The Headmaster's wife spent almost an hour afterwards mopping up and removing all traces of water.

Another visiting lecturer was the Sacristan of Westminster who came to tell us about preparations for the 1937 coronation of King George VI and Queen Elizabeth. This was after the abdication of King Edward VIII, later to become the Duke of Windsor.

Earlier, in 1936, the whole school was assembled one morning and told that King Edward VIII would be passing Moreton End on his way to Luton Hoo. We were all given a small Union Jack to wave as the King passed by. We marched out of the school and stood on the pavement for what seemed like an hour. The King's car was late. At last the cry went up, "Here he comes." A black Rolls Royce, bearing the Royal crest at the front, sped along Luton Road. We all waved our flags and someone called, "Three cheers for the King!" I looked in vain for a sight of the King but all I saw was a blur. The car didn't even slow down.

Each term, a visit of interest was arranged. A hired coach would arrive at the school at 9 o'clock to take us to the selected venue. Everyone in the school went, except Mrs Card who stayed behind. Each boy, complete with packed lunch, would happily take his place on the coach. After all, a school 'outing' was better than lessons.

Once we went to see the dress rehearsal for the Aldershot Tattoo! Another occasion took us to Hendon Air Pageant. It was here that the American parachutist, Clem Son, lost his life when his parachute failed to open; but this tragedy was not witnessed by us.

School excursions did not take us too far. After all, we didn't want to spend any longer than necessary on the coach. Consequently, visits were restricted to perhaps a tour of London, including a trip on the River Thames, or to various factories. The head boy, Randall, was unpopular at Morris's Works when he unfavourably compared their methods with Vauxhall. Once, we went round a printing works in St Albans, and another time round a hat factory in Luton. All excursions were carefully selected to be educational, and I think they were.

Sometimes, after morning break, we had fire drill. All the boys had to take part. First, we had to remove our house-shoes, then the drill itself consisted of descending from the top classroom window via an enclosed canvas chute onto the lawn below. Mr Card was always the first to go. Having first anchored one end to the classroom window-sill, he had to manoeuvre his way down the chute without anyone holding the other end. The vertical descent was about thirty feet. After that, he held the end to make the chute more taught, so that it was easier for the boys to descend. One boy, Don Hooker, usually managed to get stuck sideways half way down, and was then 'rescued' by his Headmaster.

The beginning of November was always an exciting time as November 5th drew near. The school always had a good fireworks display with a large bonfire in the field which adjoined Badminton Hall. Badminton Hall itself was of timber construction with a large gymnasium which had a pedestrian access from Luton Road near the school, and a vehicular access (of a sort) off Moreton End

Lane. Boxing was compulsory and took place there once a week. My sparring partner was Michael Hawkes, later to become Deputy Chairman of Kleinwort Benson. Both he and I were of similar size, height and weight.

The early indication of the forthcoming bonfire night's attraction was my father's lorry taking surplus firewood and odds and ends up Moreton End Lane for the bonfire. The lorry could be seen from the classroom window. On November 5th itself, the fireworks display, attended by the boys and their parents, was preceded by processions and a rather good 'Guy'. There was always a 'Parkin' made by Mrs Card, which was handed round and consumed with relish. Once, the school had a large fire balloon which floated across the sky, employing the principles of a hot air balloon. That year, there was also a splendid display of the Aurora Borealis, unusual in the south. The best fireworks display, however, was in 1938 when Mr Card's brother-in-law, Major Martin, accidentally caused a spark to drop into a box of fireworks, with very spectacular results! Badminton Hall no longer exists. It was burned down in the 1940s, not, I hasten to add, as the result of a firework display!

Looking back now, I am rather astonished at the calibre of boy who attended Moreton End School in the pre-war days leading up to 1939. Twenty percent later qualified as medical doctors and ten percent as scientists.

One boy, John Lydekker, who was one of the original five boys when the school started in 1933, was wounded at the Battle of Narvik in 1940 whilst serving with the Fleet Air Arm. He later lost his life when serving as a 2nd Lieutenant on a Canadian corvette. The captain had been blown overboard during an enemy attack and John Lydekker jumped into the water in a vain attempt to try to save him. Both were drowned. John was posthumously awarded the Distinguished Service Cross. He was the son of Captain Guy Lydekker, and a nephew of Mr John W. Lydekker of The White House, 65–69, High Street, Harpenden (*later known as The Tollgate Hotel*, now occupied by *Taylor, Walker*, solicitors). Mr John W Lydekker was, at the time of his nephew's death, Assistant Adjutant in the Home Guard.

John Lydekker's great-aunt, Miss Hilda Lydekker, lived with her sister at Harpenden Lodge, the grounds of which have recently been developed by Bovis. Harpenden Lodge had been the family home of the Lydekkers since 1857. Hilda Lydekker's father – an eminent palaeontologist and a Fellow of the Royal Society, who catalogued the vertibrate fossils of The British Museum – had married the rector of Wheathampstead's daughter in 1882. There were five children from the marriage.

Hilda was educated with her sisters, Beatrice and Helen, by a governess but her two brothers were sent to school. Eventually, only Hilda was left and she continued to live at Harpenden Lodge without any modernisation until ill-health forced her into a nursing home in 1979. Later, she entered Harpenden Memorial Hospital where she died in 1986, just six weeks short of her 101st birthday. In 1937, she had made an agreement with the then Harpenden Urban District Council that the grounds of Harpenden Lodge should be reserved as an open space. Unfortunately, Miss Lydekker never bequeathed the land to Harpenden U.D.C. and, under the terms of a later dated will, her assets passed in the main to a nephew who wished to realise their value. Hence, the development of the site with housing.

Moreton End School Football Squad (1938)
The captain, Randall, is holding the football. Michael Hawkes is on the far left. My brother is kneeling far left.

Of course, there was a good deal of snobbishness in Harpenden, not least amongst the parents. When Mr Card first started the school with his five pupils, it included a boy called Randall who was a little older than the others. Some parents approached Mr Card to say that they didn't think that Randall was good enough to be at the school, simply explaining that he did not possess the right background, and consequently they did not wish their own sons to associate with him. Notwithstanding, Mr Card accepted him and he became School Captain, excellent at sport, and a shining example to the other boys.

Other pupils who started that first term with Randall and Lydekker in 1933 also did well:

Faulkner-Lee   (became a doctor)
Perkins   (always musically gifted, became a composer)
Adams   (a scientist)
Richmond   (a farmer)

At the very beginning, the staff consisted of Mr Card and his wife, Vera, who took on the role of Matron, plus one female teacher (Miss Stretton).

During my years at the school (1936–1939), the average number of pupils was around thirty-five, of whom six boarded (including two sets of brothers, the Kime brothers, and the Chapman brothers). This would not be viable nowadays and the numbers rose to eighty-five during Mr Billinghurst's later headmastership. Girls were admitted for the first time in 1978 but only of kindergarten age (seven years). Today, I believe that there are over one hundred pupils but no longer any boarders.

Mr Card sold the school at the outbreak of the Second World War in 1939 although, to be more accurate, it was Mrs Card who had the greater hand in its sale. Her husband was virtually on the brink of a nervous breakdown and his wife sent him away on a cruise to recuperate. During the cruise, war was declared.

Mr and Mrs Card later ran a hotel in the Lake District (in the area which had originally been Mrs Card's home). She died about twenty years ago, but Mr Card survived her for a further six years. He was well into his eighties when he died.

In 1978, I met both of them at their home in Grange-over-Sands. It was a nostalgic reunion. They said that they recognised

Moreton End School
37 boys at the school on 3rd April 1939
Below: The photographer's caption, pasted on the back of the print.

April 3rd 1939   MORETON END SCHOOL   Oliver G Harvey, Portrait Photographer
35 High Street, Harpenden, Tel: 807

Back Row : Barlow – Jeremy – Carter(Jnr) – Wace – Samuels – Hurt – Webster(Ralph) – Downey

Hooker – Garrod – Richmond (Peter) – Auerbach –Webster(Brian) –Greaves.

Centre : Hawkes –Carter(Snr) –Jones – Williams –Isaacs – Adams – Kime(Snr) –Boughey –Perkins

Richmond(John) –Davidson (jnr) –Ross– Gregory –Johnson – Robinson.

Front : Kime(Jnr) –Fatty Chapman – Faulkner Lee – Randall – Mr. McDonald – Mrs. Card –Mr. Card

Miss Morgan – Mr. Ritchie – Hill –Chapman (Snr) –Childs(Brian)–Woods.

me from my young son, aged seven, who accompanied me. Apparently, he very much resembled me at the same age. They made me and my family very welcome and I could not help but notice how much Mr Card had mellowed from those early days of his headmastership of Moreton End School.

The headmasters of Moreton End School are set out below. Some dates are approximate:

Mr V.E.H. Card	1933–1939
Mr O'Hara	1939–1940 (died at the school)
Mrs O'Hara	1941–1945
Mr Codrington	1945–1950
Mr Billinghurst	1950–1973
Temporary Headmaster	1973 (appointed by the Principal, P. J. Langham)
Mr R.A. Cansfield	1974–1990
Mrs Angela Clements	1990–1995

Allowing for the change of name to "The Harpenden Preparatory School", 2003 is the 70th anniversary of the founding of the school.

CHAPTER SIX

Salad Days

By the 1930s, Harpenden had begun to develop. Already E.C and F.H. Jarvis had developed West Common Way and had now commenced development of a 45-acre site known as "The Carisbrooke Building Estate" which embraced Lyndhurst Drive, Elliswick Road, Carisbrooke and adjoining roads. Cattons were building in the north of Harpenden – Park Mount, Park Hill, and Kinsbourne Green. Many houses were for renting. The other major local builders, Claridge of Hall Brothers, concentrated in the Overstone Road and Dalkeith Road areas.

In Fallows Green at the top of Ox Lane, the large house where Ellen Terry, the actress, once lived, was pulled down to make way for a new estate developed by my father's firm, H.E. Webster Ltd. The houses were individually designed by a local architect, H. Hopson-Hill, and this combination also built new private houses in Redbourn Lane, Sauncey Avenue and Wheathampstead Road. Most houses were for private clients. Few were built speculatively.

By the mid 1930s, the economy was beginning to improve and prosperity was anticipated in Harpenden. Rates were eleven shillings (*55p*) in the pound; the charge for electricity was 2½d (*1p*) per unit for heating and 6d (*2½p*) per unit for lighting. The price of gas was 1 shilling (*5p*) per therm.

A few retired civil servants and colonial people began to settle in Harpenden and join the wealthy industrialists and businessmen already living there. Most of those domiciled in the large houses had live-in servants – probably a cook, housemaid, and gardener/handyman. Even houses in the more unfashionable areas such as Willoughby Road had a live-in housemaid. These were generally young girls from the north-east who wanted to escape the poverty stricken areas of their home towns, and moved down south to go 'into service'.

Much of the local working-class populace, who worked as farm labourers, shop assistants and in the building trade, lived mainly in the Southdown area of Harpenden (famous for its 'skew' railway bridge); but also in the out-lying districts where houses were cheaply rented. Very few of the working-class owned their own homes. The native dialect of Harpenden, or indeed Hertfordshire, was more prevalent during this period. This dialect can sometimes still be heard today and is similar to that used by the late Bernard Miles (Lord Miles) when he portrayed a country farm worker in a solo monologue. I suppose this is the accent I took with me to Moreton End School when I was asked to improve my speech!

All in all, despite some hardships experienced by the poorer people, the middle to late 1930s can be classed as prosperous. If you were fairly well off, you could enjoy a genteel life. The local butcher or grocer would deliver goods to your home after you had placed an order. Your cook would prepare your meals; your maid would do much of your housework and bring refreshments to your guests. Whilst her husband was attending to business in London, the lady of the house could perhaps visit Marion Chew in Leyton Road to try on the latest gown, or H. Temple (milliners of Leyton Road) for a fashionable new hat. Afternoon tea could be obtained in the tea rooms above Jos. E West (bakery) or Bunty's, and dinner at the Kirkwick Hotel *(now the Hanover)*. A very pleasant life for many but if you were from the working-class, that was a different story . . .

I recently came across details of a prescription dated July 15th 1939, addressed to Mrs Webster, Bowers House. It was from J. Busby Ltd (established 1869) of 12, High Street, and came in its own envelope accompanying the medicine in question. I had quite forgotten that in pre-war days it was common practice for the local chemist to deliver your prescription to your home, if asked to. Naturally, the cost would go onto your account. The firm of J. Busby Ltd was sold in 1991 and I have since wondered why the name of such an old established pharmacist was changed to "Springfield Pharmacy".

After a while, I settled in at Moreton End and made new friends – some remaining to this day. I remember having been quite friendly with a boy called Jones – Tubby Jones to his friends on account of being rather portly. One day, during the school holidays, he invited me to visit him at home and gave me his address in Milton Road.

The day duly arrived and I found that he lived in one of the grand Edwardian houses on the left-hand side (going from Station Road). His mother announced that we were to stay on the top floor (the house had three floors) in Tubby's den, but at 11 o'clock

No. *H 1862* Date *15 - - 39*

The Prescription.

Mrs Webster.

Dispensed by

J. Busby, Ltd.,

Dispensing Chemists,

12. High Street,

Harpenden.

Established 1869. *Tel. No. 104.*

'SANATOGEN' (Trade Mark) The Famous Brand of tonic food. Energises the nerves and builds up the body cells. 5 sizes—Tins 2/3 to 10/9. Family Jar 19/9.

'GENASPRIN' (Trade Mark) *The Safe Brand of Aspirin*—guaranteed free from all impurities. In bottles 27 Tablets 1/3, 50 Tablets 2/-, 100 Tablets (including pocket carrier) 3/6. Also Handy Tubes 6d.

'GENOZO' (Trade Mark) (BRAND) **Tooth Paste** prepared to the prescription of an eminent doctor and a distinguished bacteriologist. Two flavours—Standard (Peppermint) and Lemon. In tubes 6d., 1/-, 1/6.

'GENATOSAN' (Trade Mark) **PRODUCTS — YOUR ASSURANCE OF PURITY.**

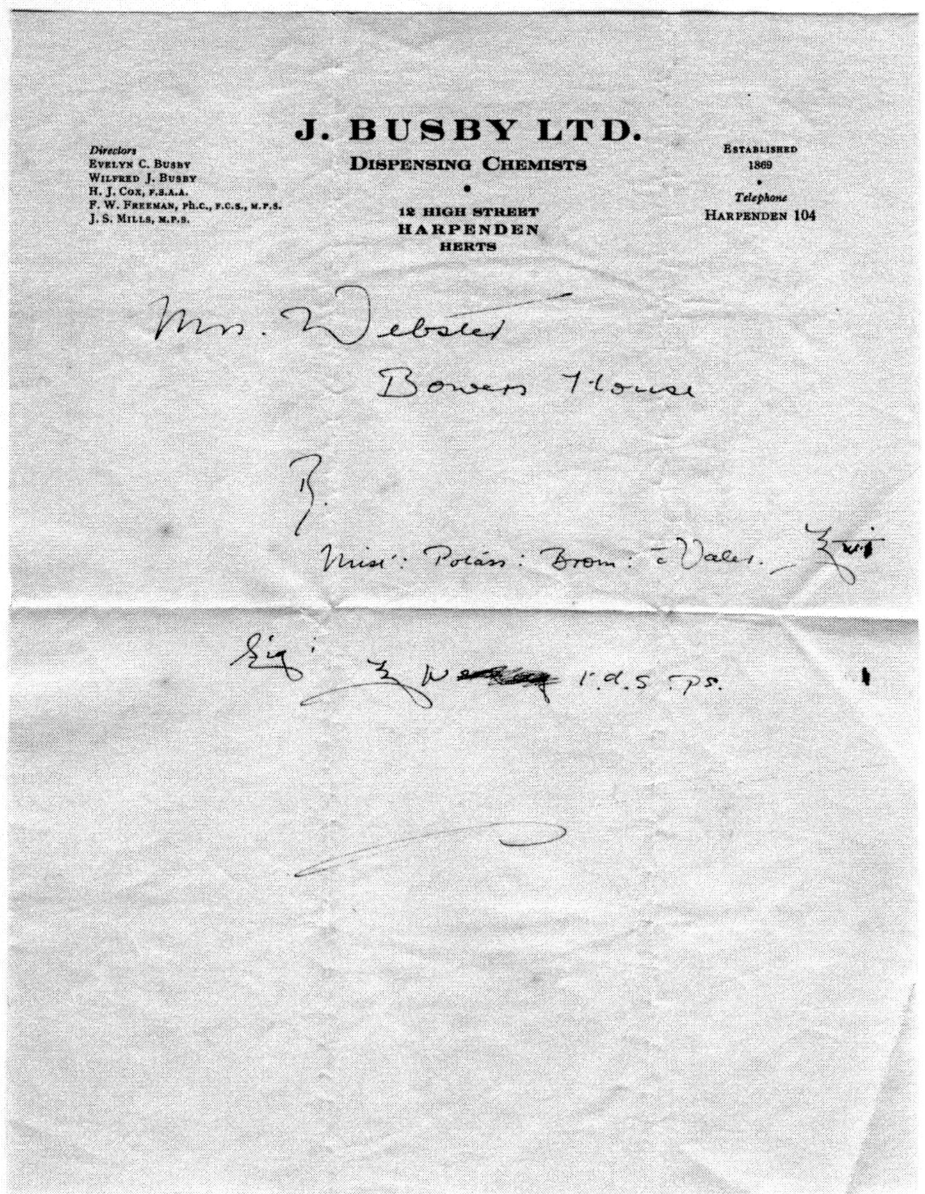

A Prescription

Messrs. Busby of 12 High Street dispensed and delivered this prescription to my mother at Bowers House in 1939.

we were to go downstairs for lemonade.

So, at the appointed hour, having spent the morning being shown Tubby's things – hobbies, collections, etc. – I went with him downstairs to the morning room where his mother was waiting. She rang a bell and a maid appeared, traditionally dressed in black with a white apron and cap, about forty years of age, dark-haired and slim. Mrs Jones then said we would be taking morning break in the garden, ordered coffee for herself and lemonade for Tubby and me. We sat on garden chairs at a rustic table enjoying the morning sunshine. The only sound above our conversation was that of the birds singing. Shortly, the maid appeared carrying a silver tray on which was placed a coffee pot, milk jug and sugar basin, cup and saucer, together with a large jug of lemonade and two glasses. She went back into the house, to emerge again carrying a jar of biscuits and some side plates. The lemonade was home-made, produced from lemonade crystals with a few lemon slices popped onto the top. The maid said, "Thank you, Madam." I don't know why she was thanking Mrs Jones; it should surely have been the other way round! I was so impressed, I have never forgotten it.

At Bowers House, we didn't have a maid. My mother did her own cooking but she had a 'daily' (Mrs Bracey) who came to do the housework. Mrs Bracey was middle-aged, portly and red faced. I thought it a shame that she had to come out 'charring' in order to supplement her husband's income. I think he worked as a builder's labourer. She always seemed to be out of breath, and at the end of her day's work (which finished in the mid-afternoon), she had a long walk home to Batford.

Although we didn't have a maid at Bowers House, we had a

ghost! At least, my mother always swore that she had seen it, not once but several times. The first time was early in 1938 when my father was lying in bed desperately ill suffering from pneumonia. These were the days before the introduction of 'M & B' tablets, and there was little anyone could do except wait for the crisis of the illness, when the patient either survived with the fever subsiding, or died.

My mother had moved into a separate bedroom when my father became ill and, at the same time, had asked his mother (my grandmother) to stay with us for a few days until the worst was over. We had plenty of rooms so there was no problem in putting her up. On the second night after my grandmother's arrival, my mother claimed that at about 2.00 a.m. she awoke from a worrying, fitful sleep to find a little old lady dressed in grey, eighteenth century clothes, with a small white cap on her curled grey hair. She was standing at the foot of my mother's bed with her index finger raised to her lips. "Ssh," she whispered, "don't worry. He's going to be all right." The next morning, my grandmother arose early and went into my father's bedroom. He was breathing normally and the fever had passed. I well remember hearing my grandmother excitedly going into my mother's room to give her the news of my father's recovery. It was later that day that mother told the story of her night-time visitor and it never wavered in its telling.

I have read elsewhere about the ghost of Bowers House. Could it have been Polly Stirling whose name is etched on the window-pane of the large bedroom window which we used as a sports room? Although mother claimed she saw the ghost several times afterwards and dressed exactly as before, it never spoke to her again.

By this time, of course, Edward VIII had abdicated the throne in favour of his brother and we had had King George VI's Coronation in 1937. Harpenden made an excellent job of the celebrations, having had a practice for the Jubilee two years before. Decorations and lanterns (still kept from the Jubilee) were brought out again and the village enjoyed a repeat performance. This time, however, the celebrations included a Coronation Tea, enjoyed on long trestle tables and benches set out on the Broadway Hall indoor market.

One special treat for me was to be taken by my father to London on the Sunday morning before the Coronation, to watch the rehearsal of the coach procession. We had to get off by 5 o'clock in the morning and there was a large crowd. I sat on my father's shoulders about six deep in the crowd and couldn't see all that much. My father bought a small periscope, on sale by the street vendors, but it didn't seem to work very well. However, I do remember the golden State Coach being drawn by the grey mares, even though the real King and Queen were not inside it.

My father's firm continued to prosper and had about fifty employees. From this number, he was able to form a football team called "Webster's Wasps Football Club". The team played soccer in a field at Hatching Green. This field was owned by a well-known theatrical producer, Mr Ben Travers, who lived at West Common. Mr Travers achieved fame from his Whitehall Theatre farces starring Tom Walls, Ralph Lynn and Alfred Drayton. Incidentally, Alfred Drayton also lived in Harpenden during the war and he, with beaming face and shiny bald head, could often be seen in The Cock public house in the High Street.

Webster's Wasps wore black shorts and mustard yellow shirts bearing the insignia 'W.F.C.' over the left breast pocket.

The team comprised:

Jack Grey, Peter Titmus, John Wood, Gerry Lawrence, 'Jammy' Godfrey, George (Spinney) Fox, Ted Gray, Bill Batchelor, Frank Hough, Les Gillow, and Arthur 'Bricky' Ward.

Later, Bob Gay, a painter and decorator, joined the team. A small man but a nimble player with the ball. I am uncertain whether anyone of the team is still alive. I know that 'Jammy' Godfrey, a fine centre-half, lost his life during the 1939–45 war. 'Spinney' Fox, a carpenter, died about twenty years ago.

The pinnacle of Webster's Wasps' achievements was the final of the Pratt Cup in 1939 on the Common, when they defeated Harpenden Town 1 – 0. I remember the cheering afterwards and, in the gathering dusk, the speeches made by the captain and then by the scorer of the winning goal. When it came to my father's turn to say a few words, he stood on a wooden box and started to speak but the crowd no longer seemed interested and melted away. After all, he hadn't done anything to win the match. So he got down again and said nothing more. The teams were together only for the 1938 and 1939 seasons in which they also won the Bingham Cox Cup before disbanding at the outbreak of war.

There being no television, entertainment for the average household was provided by the wireless, the cinema, or a 'show' at the theatre. Once a year, we also had the 'Stattie' Fair – always exciting to watch its arrival on the second Sunday in September. We used to wonder on which part of the Common it would take place and then, once the various roundabouts, stalls and side-shows were being erected, to try to guess what they would be. The

The Church in Leyton Road Before its Conversion into the Regent Cinema.
(opposite).

fair itself only lasted two days, on the Tuesday and Wednesday evenings. This quickly passed and, whilst watching the dismantling, we realised with dismay that we had to wait a whole year for the fair to come again. I do not recollect in pre-war days there being a fair at Easter, Whitsuntide or August Bank Holiday, as there is today.

We had two cinemas: the Austral (already mentioned) and the Regent, the latter having been converted by H.E. Webster Ltd. from a church into a cinema. It was owned by Mr Latty who lived in Bowers Way. The cinema was situated in Leyton Road on the

When the cinema closed in 1960, Anscombes used the building as their furniture department.

right-hand side of Anscombes. In the 1960s, when the cinema industry began to decline, the building was acquired by Anscombes for their furniture department.

In 1938, the film "Sixty Glorious Years", starring Anna Neagle as Queen Victoria, was showing at the Austral. Mr Card deemed this a suitable film for the pupils of Moreton End School to see. Consequently, he booked seats for us in the first rows of the balcony – it would have been unseemly for us to go downstairs in the cheaper seats – and we walked in single file along the pavement from the school to the cinema in time for the afternoon's showing. I presume that the Headmaster saw this as a history lesson.

The school play, always a feature of Moreton End, was performed at Rothamsted Manor the same year. The play itself was more of a sketch really, but it was nostalgic to go along to the manor house recently, which I had not visited since 1931 when my mother had taken me to an auction sale of its contents. The house, originally the home of Sir John Lawes, was sold in 1931 and acquired by Rothamsted Experimental Station. I still have a small French carriage clock which my mother acquired at the auction.

Harpenden did not possess a theatre, although there were two in Luton – the Alma and the Grand. Occasionally, however, the Harpenden Amateur Dramatic Society would put on a show at the Public Hall. During the winter of 1938/39 the Society produced a pantomime. One of the principals taking part was Mr Edward (Ted) Bentley of the grocer's family. Boys of Moreton End School were invited to auditions to play the part of the seven dwarfs in a scene from "Snow White". This was considered to be very topical because Walt Disney's film had recently been released. My brother, Brian, got the part of Dopey – mainly, I think, because he looked right for the part.

I wonder how many people remember some of the 'characters' when Harpenden was still a village:

'Jesus' Jackson, with snow-white beard and hair, always dressed in shorts and sandals, riding a tricycle, yet a university professor of mathematics.

1938/1939 *Winter's Pantomime at Harpenden Public Hall*
My brother is 7th from the right. Mr. Edward Bentley, in evening tails and hatless,
is on the centre right of the picture.

*Dr Ross, who always drove a Rover car, lived in Station Road, with his
practice (in partnership with Dr MacLean) in the old surgery next to
Mary Ellens.*

*Miss Helen Finnie herself, proprietor of Mary Ellens (later pulled down
to make way for a modern, ugly building called "Inn on the Green",
which is really rather akin to a pub).*

I remember seeing Miss Finnie in her pre-war days, carrying a
large wicker basket covered with a cloth, the handle over her

forearm. She was walking along Leyton Road heading towards Rothamsted Avenue, where she would deliver in person home-made cakes and scones to those in the large houses who had ordered them.

Miss Helen Finnie was a large lady, usually dressed in tweed skirt and twin-set, but a lady in every sense of the word. Originally from Scotland, she and her sister had started the business in the 1920s, principally to sell small tea cakes and scones. The building was constructed to give the appearance of mock Tudor, with timbers half-exposed and leaded light front windows. Above the fascia, a notice proclaimed "Lunch – Tea – Supper". Its raised fascia cleverly disguised the corrugated iron roof. Inside, a brick-built fireplace normally contained a roaring log fire in wintertime which made the café very cosy indeed. Included with the fireplace was a handsome oak over-mantel containing a quotation from Chaucer picked out in red paint. I wonder what happened to it?

After her sister moved back to Scotland, Helen Finnie ran the business herself until she retired to 43, Milton Road in about 1968, when "Mary Ellen" was pulled down to make way for "The Inn on the Green". In addition to delicious home-made cakes, Mary Ellen was famous for its soups and savoury pancakes. A very nice, inexpensive café, open until 9.00 or 10.00 p.m., where you could be assured of a good quality meal. Even during the war, Miss Finnie's savoury pancakes, made from dried egg, were recognised as the finest to be had.

Helen Finnie also took a very active part in the life of the community. Her café was a popular meeting place and some societies held their meetings there. She was also a member of the Poetry Circle. Her death in 1987 marked the end of an era.

Mary Ellens

Distribution of Gas Masks
The distribution of gas masks took place in 1938 at the Old Public Hall. In this picture the author can be seen on the left, whilst his younger brother on the right is being fitted for his gas mask. In the centre is Basil Greaves, friend of my brother, and a fellow pupil at Moreton End School.

By 1938, a few rumblings reached us of what was happening in Europe – particularly in Germany. No one, it seemed, was particularly alarmed. Even if the newspapers were supressing the news, as had happened with the story of King Edward VIII's association with Mrs Wallis Simpson, there was nothing to get really alarmed about. Germany might have been a world away as far as some people were concerned, and although the thought of war crossed some people's minds, there appeared still to be a pleasantly relaxed attitude to life. After all, didn't we possess the largest navy in the world?

The Old Public Hall
Located near the entrance to Rothamsted Park in Leyton Road. In recent times the Hall has been used for registering births and deaths.

To most boys at Moreton End, Adolf Hitler and Benito Mussolini were comic cartoon characters, always portrayed in the daily newspapers, strutting and saluting and, even more alarmingly, on the Gaumont-British newsreels which accompanied every film shown at the Austral or Regent cinemas.

At the crisis time of Münich and the war scare when Germany invaded Czechoslovakia in 1938, gas masks were distributed to all civilians, and most children knew about gas mask drill. In Harpenden, the fitting of gas masks took place in the old Public Hall in Leyton Road (*recently the domicile of the Citizens' Advice Bureau*). Very young children were issued with colourful gas masks shaped like Mickey Mouse.

As we went into 1939, the relaxed attitude to life continued. The calm before the storm! Entertainment revolved around Flanagan and Allen, George Formby, Gracie Fields, Will Hay, and Snow White and the Seven Dwarfs. Bandleaders like Bert Ambrose, Geraldo, and Joe Loss were at the height of popularity, and a vocalist named Al Bowlly was the Tom Jones of 1939.

Popular song-wise, nearly everyone seemed to be whistling or humming "South of the Border, down Mexico way", "Run, Rabbit, Run", "When the Poppies Bloom Again", "Underneath the Spreading Chestnut Tree". Schoolboys had certain parodies of these songs, one of which went:

"Underneath the spreading chestnut tree,
Neville Chamberlain said to me . . .
If you want to get your gas mask free,
Join the blinking A.R.P."

Another parody of the song from "Snow White and the Seven Dwarfs", although this was developed towards the end of 1939, went like this:

"Whistle while you work.
Mussolini bought a shirt.
Hitler wore it,
Goering tore it.
Wasn't he a twerp?"

A West End show in London, with dinner for two afterwards at the Dorchester Hotel, could be had for under a fiver. Salad days indeed!

CHAPTER SEVEN

The Threat of Nazi Germany

In the Easter term of 1939, our school outing was a visit to the dockyards at Chatham. The Headmaster, Mr Card, arranged this not without some difficulty. The fleet was now being prepared for war and Mr Card had to seek and obtain special permission from the Admiralty before the outing could take place. Eventually, all the formalities were completed, and on a fine Spring day we set off in our hired coach. When we arrived at the dockyards, we inspected many ships from the quayside. Much activity was taking place, but it was difficult to see whether the ships were being prepared for war engagement or normal peacetime repair. We were allowed to go on board a small corvette, which was the highlight of our visit.

By the beginning of the summer in 1939, people were being encouraged to build their own air-raid shelters, not that there was any real danger of war breaking out – but just in case. Mr Card decided that Moreton End should have one. This was located at the rear of the school lawn on which so many prize-giving days had been held in the past. My father's firm was employed to build two shelters, constructed of concrete and built underground. I do not think that they were ever used for a real bomb attack, but we enjoyed air-raid practice because this reduced the time remaining for lessons. Once, a boy named Peter Kime lit a fire in one of the shelters and caused some consternation. That was the only real excitement they ever produced.

As the summer wore on, people were divided in opinion on the terrifying prospects of war with Germany. Many adults followed the theory of Neville Chamberlain's policy of appeasement and shrugged off the thought of war with an 'old Hitler's bluffing' complacency; they firmly rejected the pessimism of men like Winston Churchill and Hugh Dalton, who had seen nothing but danger in the Nazi way of life. My father thought that England would settle with Germany without going to war because, he argued, England was so unprepared that it could not possibly engage Germany in war. Apart from the navy, England had little or no air force and very few troops who could be quickly mobilised.

In most places in Britain, Sunday 3rd September 1939 dawned fine and sunny. Harpenden was no exception. There was even something vaguely romantic about the early autumn leaves blowing along the pavements and the super-charged atmosphere – almost melancholy – as people awaited the expected pronouncement by the Prime Minister at 11.00 a.m.

Surprisingly, the churches were not very full, for there was a great deal of activity amongst the community. Adults were helping to dig the deep air-raid shelters on the Greens opposite Bowers Parade and Leyton Green, and at East Common. My friend, Alan Bell, and I – both eleven year olds – were filling sand

Preparing for War
Digging the air raid shelter on the green opposite Bowers Parade, 3rd September 1939. The work was carried out by hand, and the surplus excavated soil carried away by horse and cart (no J.C.B.'s or dumper tractor in those days).

bags along Bowers Parade, which were to be used for the shelter being dug on the Green between Bowers Parade and the Cock Inn.

A few minutes before 11 o'clock, work stopped and people congregated around wherever there was a wireless set. Along Bowers Parade itself there was a parked car which had a radio (a rare luxury for those days), and the owner opened the doors wide so that those standing near could hear Alvar Liddel announce that the British ultimatum for the German withdrawal from Poland had expired, and that no reply had been received from the German government; consequently, a broadcast of grave importance would follow at approximately 11.15 a.m. This, of course, was the famous Chamberlain speech to the nation, ending with his solemn, faltering words: "I have to tell you that I have received no such undertaking from the German authorities, and that a state of war now exists between our two countries." In some ways, it all came as an anti-climax because, by now, people had come to expect it.

Work resumed after about fifteen minutes, but many of the younger children who had been helping to fill sandbags went home with their fathers. Fathers, in turn, wanted to be with their wives. It was a time for the family to be together.

CHAPTER EIGHT

Harpenden at War

So the anti-climax continued: as did the phoney war.

Apart from the first night, when the air-raid sirens sounded at the first sighting of an aircraft overhead (which turned out to be British), the air-raid shelters were seldom used afterwards. Visions of explosions shaking the ground, of buildings crumbling into rubble and ruin, of the fire brigades and ambulances scurrying through the smoke-filled streets of Harpenden, and destruction beneath the drone of German bombers, soon faded. However, the period of the phoney war – or 'Sitzkrieg' – between September 1939 and May 1940 enabled the people of Harpenden to carry out preparations for a real war should an enemy invasion or air attack take place.

The A.R.P. (Air Raid Precaution Services) had been formed in 1938 together with the W.V.S. (Women's Voluntary Services), and allied organisations became firmly established. Two Harpenden businessmen, Mr F.N. Gingell and Mr H.C. Williamson, were appointed Controller and Deputy Controller of the A.R.P. (W2 sector). The headquarters of this arm of civil defence was the Park Hall at the entrance to Rothamsted Park. The early volunteers were enthusastic and, before uniforms were issued, turned up in tweed jackets and old flannel bags. Part of the task of the A.R.P. was to ensure that the blackout was secure at night time. One resident on Topstreet Way was fined £1 in September 1942 for having an unscreened light during the blackout.

At the beginning of the war, my father, as a builder, was classed as being in a 'reserved occupation', but he joined the A.R.P. as a warden and was given a badge. I accompanied him on one occasion to an exercise on the grassed area behind the Park Hall where Mr Gingell was to give a demonstration on the use of a stirrup pump in extinguishing an incendiary bomb. We stood back and waited expectantly. Quite a crowd had gathered to see Mr Gingell emerge with a bucket of water, a stirrup pump, and an incendiary. He was short, inclined to be portly and a little pompous (not unlike Captain Mainwaring of "Dad's Army" fame), and full of enthusiasm. Unfortunately, something went wrong and no water came out. The crowd laughed and went home. Red faced, so did Mr Gingell.

There was no doubt, however, that he was energetic and put a good deal of effort into his A.R.P. work. He had the charisma and personality to generate enthusiasm amongst the wardens whilst also devoting time as a member of Harpenden Urban District Council, and to his main job which was Managing Director of Harpenden Dairies whose offices, shop and depot were situated in Station Road. (The premises later formed an extension to the Post Office). Some years later, both F.N. Gingell and H.C. Williamson were awarded the M.B.E. for their work in

Harpenden. Mr Henry Cecil Williamson lived in Harpenden until his death in April 1992; Mr Gingell had pre-deceased him a quarter of a century earlier.

Even cigarette cards were issued, depicting air-raid precautions. I remember a series by Churchman's which showed *"How to remove an incendiary bomb with a long-handled hoe and a coke scoop"*. Another card gave details of *"How to equip your refuge room or air raid shelter"* and yet another depicted how easy it was to build a bomb-splinter-proof wall!

Whether any of this advice ever came to be used, it is difficult to know. Harpenden certainly had its share of incendiary bombs dropped by German aircraft later in the war. One night a 'Molotov Cocktail' of incendiaries came through the roof of 1, Bowers Parade – but was quickly put out. On another occasion, unexploded incendiary bombs fell on the field below Sir John Lawes School. The 'butterfly' tops of their tail fins could easily be seen sticking out of the ground. They were quite tiny bombs and looked inoffensive. Boys cycled down the footpath by the London North Eastern railway line to collect souvenirs from the field where Waverley Close is now situated. A very dangerous practice, but nothing very much was thought about any danger involved.

Another branch of civil defence was the Home Guard. In May 1940, Winston Churchill became Prime Minister and he, together with Mr Anthony Eden, encouraged the formation of civil defence units in every village and town in England. Harpenden formed its own Home Guard under the command of Colonel West who worked as an accountant for a bank. He had held a commission in the Army during the first World War in 1914–1918.

In the early days of 1940, the Home Guard was known as the L.D.V. (Local Defence Volunteers). Later, the unit in Harpenden became the No. 2 Platoon Home Guard. It was, of course, difficult to find recruits, since all the fit and able young men had been called up to serve in the armed forces. There were only those left who had failed their medical, those in 'reserved occupations', and the older members of the community. However, no one thought of them as being a 'Dad's Army'. They were issued with denim uniforms and some rifles and held manoeuvres regularly. They published their own News Sheet, "The Perimeter Post" and, I believe, started the Harpenden Ferndale Cricket Club.

A 'de-contamination' centre was formed in Thompson Close in the Council yard. This was in case of an enemy gas attack. Black painted pillar boxes with horizontal slits were positioned at strategic places. These were to create smoke in the event of an enemy attack, the idea being to ignite oil-soaked rags stuffed inside. I never saw one actually used.

A Women's Land Army was formed and land girls, dressed in their peculiar jodhpurs, worked on the farms of Harpenden. People were encouraged to 'dig for victory' by turning their gardens into small allotments. The Harpenden Potato Club was formed and in 1942 produced 50 tons from 140 plots, giving an average of 7 cwts from each 5-pole plot.

Harpenden Common was cleared of its gorse bushes and was sown with wheat and barley. In fact, it was some time after the war before the Common was restored to its present grassland. Many of the smaller businesses closed whilst the principal and staff joined up or went to work for a Ministry office.

Another problem caused by the call-up into the forces was the shortage of teachers at the local schools. Initially, some schools taught a kind of correspondence course where the pupils collected set homework from the school and returned it for correction at the end of the week. A most unsatisfactory method of education, but after a while things became easier with the appointment of lady teachers and even retired headmasters.

Many of the children in those early days had been evacuated from London, arriving at Harpenden Station complete with identification label and gas mask contained in a brown cardboard box, worn with a strap over the shoulder. I remember seeing these children – most of them poorly dressed – carrying cheap little suitcases, walking two or three abreast down Station Road. They were accompanied by a few officials and some of the parents, to congregate outside the Harpenden Public Hall to await billeting in Harpenden.

At the outbreak of war, Hertfordshire became the reception area for evacuees, both official and unofficial, from London – for the bulk of Hertfordshire was a 'reception area' and prior plans had been made for the acceptance and billeting of evacuees. So, the first few months of wartime witnessed large-scale evacuation of children from vulnerable areas, but, during the calm and comparative peace of the 'phoney war', many returned home before the danger of bombing became a reality.

Shortly after the outbreak of war, my brother and I went to live with our grandparents in Derbyshire. I think my father believed that there was some danger of aerial bomb attacks on Harpenden due to its proximity to London. However, we returned in early 1940 to find that certain changes had occurred.

Firstly, my parents had moved into No. 3 flat at Bowers House, having vacated the large, main house due, I believe, to the fear of having troops billeted on them. No. 3 flat is situated on the first floor at the north east end of Bowers House, with a staircase access from the outside pathway.

Secondly, having reached my eleventh birthday the previous year (in 1939), it was decided to send me to a new school. This was a matter of some urgency since I had received practically no education whilst I had been staying in Derbyshire, where the correspondence homework method, mentioned earlier, was widely practised.

Moreton End School had been sold to Mr O'Hara and I was to be sent to St Albans Modern School (*now Verulam School*), which had opened in 1936 under the head-ship of a young Mr R.F. Bradshaw, M.A., himself in his thirties. I travelled daily on the train – a ten minute journey from Harpenden Station – and walked from St Albans Station to the school in Brampton Road. The steam trains were rarely late. The carriages were divided up into individual compartments with upholstered bench-type seats, accommodating six abreast each side of the compartment. The windows contained an opening sash operated by a leather strap; a criss-cross mesh of cord holding luggage in place. If there were no adult passengers in the compartment, a favourite occupation during the ten minute journey was to see who could get up into the luggage rack and remain there in a prone position for the remainder of the journey. Since the steam trains ran almost always on time, the journey was sometimes used for putting last minute touches to our homework. Women had taken over many of the men's jobs and there were often female train guards who wore a navy blue jacket and skirt. There were also women bus drivers and conductors, the latter being affectionately known as 'Clippies'.

For me, school had to continue in a completely new wartime atmosphere of blackouts, food rationing and air-raid sirens. It was also mandatory to carry your gas mask (in its cardboard box) and identity card wherever you went. A popular hobby amongst schoolboys was collecting and swapping Army badges and buttons. Packed lunches were taken to school. There was no school dining room, although a small bottle of milk – about one third of a pint – could be purchased for 3d *(1½p)* and the meal eaten in the main hall. The only alternative was to go to the "British Restaurant" in Hatfield Road, where an unappetising plain meal of meat and two vegetables could be bought. I only tried this once, preferring to chat over lunch with my school friends in the main hall. One particular friend, I remember, ate picalilli sandwiches every day, the bright yellow of the contents contrasting sharply with everyone else's sandwiches.

The complete austerity of wartime and the total lack of even simple luxuries did not seem to worry me a great deal. I just accepted the situation and did as I was told; the idea of complaining did not occur because it was unpatriotic to do so. As in other parts of Britain, most things were on ration for which coupons or dockets were required. Cigarettes were difficult to obtain and were often sold loose, each customer being rationed to perhaps five or ten. In order to do this, the proprietor of the tobacco/sweet shop would open a packet of twenty cigarettes and split it up into four lengths of five. It was necessary for the customer to either take an envelope into the shop for carrying the cigarettes or to walk out with them loose in the hand. I remember H. Firbank, tobacconist of Leyton Green, frequently adopted this system of cigarette rationing. (The premises of H. Firbank is now occupied by a ladies' hairdressing salon).

The large department store, Anscombes, sold 'utility' furniture and linens, much of which was of a higher quality than can be obtained today, but these could not be purchased without the requisite number of coupons.

Some commodities in the food line were difficult to obtain, but there was always someone prepared to exchange one item for another, and people managed. One Harpenden shopkeeper was fined £3 (plus £3 costs) in September 1942 for overcharging for eggs.

Christmastide was the most difficult. Turkeys were almost unobtainable, and if a family managed to get hold of a chicken, they were considered to be very fortunate indeed. They were always 'under the counter' and needed to be ordered months in advance. There was a shortage of fruit during the war days. Bananas were completely unobtainable and any greengrocer who had a delivery of oranges quickly sold out to a waiting queue, limiting each customer to four oranges. The village itself had three main greengrocers: Messrs. Fells, O'Dells in Station Road, and another shop at 100, High Street run by Mr J. Stanley. Of these, J. Stanley seemed to obtain consignments of oranges more frequently than the other two. Jim Stanley, however, was a better dance band pianist than a greengrocer and he quickly tired of serving oranges to a seemingly inexhaustible queue. He used to say, "I'm fed up serving oranges", and would walk away into the back of the shop. Happily, his wife would come to the rescue and serve the remainder of those waiting.

It was Jim Stanley's son, Gordon, who introduced me to a

The Bowling Alley

The Southdown area of Harpenden, known locally as 'The Bowling Alley'. The picture shows "The Queens Head" public house. Obscured by the hedge the premises of Bandy (cycle maker) and Simpson (hairdressers) were to be found. In the background is the Skew Bridge.

barber's shop in the Bowling Alley of Southdown Road. There were a few shops on the north side of Skew Bridge, one of which was owned by a Mr Simpson (no relation to Tom Chambers's assistant, but whose prices were similar, i.e. 6d (2½p) for a haircut). Next door, Mr W. Bandy – a former cycling champion but now middle-aged and portly – ran a cycle shop where bikes were built and repaired.

Although I ventured into the dark interior of Mr Simpson's

hairdressing shop, I avoided going anywhere near Heath Road at the rear, because a few years previously there had been an epidemic of diphtheria which had affected the occupants of a couple of houses. Even when travelling along Queens Road, I would hold my breath when passing the end of Heath Road lest I breathed in any lingering germs. The Bowling Alley was considered (both pre-war and immediately post-war) to be a poorer area of Harpenden and, to the ignorant, myself included, was thus a harbinger of diseases and germs. (That other plague of the 1930s, scarlet fever, required a note pinned to the front door to the effect that someone in the house had gone down with it. I remember such a case in Willoughby Road). The row of shops by the Skew Bridge was eventually demolished to make way for a brand new block of flats and maisonettes called "Bowling Close".

In Europe, the Germans, building up their tremendous offensive, had swept through Belgium, Holland and France, and we heard of the miraculous evacuation of Dunkirk during the summer of 1940. Despite all this, I could never really visualise England losing the war. I think the comradeship, kindness and determination of the people everywhere had a great deal to do with my confidence. The speeches of Winston Churchill were also tremendously inspiring and the part of one which always stuck in my mind was the speech which included, "…Hitler knows that he has to break us on this island, or lose the war."

Historians and writers of war memoirs have since proved how desperately close to defeat England was during the Battle of Britain in September 1940, when the incredible bravery of "the Few" and the endeavours of the factory workers to provide enough Spitfires, Hurricanes, and Blenheims, enabled England to vanquish the invincible Luftwaffe!

The number of times that the residents of Harpenden saw enemy action during the war could be counted, if not on one hand, certainly on two. I vividly remember the day the Germans bombed Vauxhall Motors in Luton. It was a Friday – a black day indeed – and during the daytime Vauxhalls was targeted because they were making 'Churchill' tanks. A few bombers flew back over Harpenden Common and discharged their deadly cargo there. I remember flinging myself flat onto the grass and looking up at the black crosses painted on the underside of the aircrafts' wings, not knowing whether or not they were still loaded with bombs. One bomb fell in the grounds of Aldwickbury School, then a 50-room Victorian mansion owned by Mrs Hett. No one was hurt, but a crater remained there for a long while. The Hett family – wealthy ship owners – had lived in the house for forty years but it was the first time they had had a bomb in their gardens. Mind you, they had twenty acres! Later, a house near the bottom of Crabtree Lane was two-thirds demolished by a bomb, killing the occupants. One of the German Dornier bombers was shot down and parts were to be seen the following day strewn amongst the trees lining Bowers Heath Lane which was the main route from Batford to Kimpton. I saw the pilot's boots hanging from a tree.

On another occasion, a German bomber crashed at Gustard Wood, killing some of the crew. It never occurred to us as schoolboys what a macabre pursuit we followed when we cycled over to the scene of some of these crashes, hoping to glean as many souvenirs as the military custodians, guarding the crashed plane, would allow.

A German plane was also shot down over Harpenden and a couple of parachutists bailed out, to land on a farm on the outskirts. A teenage boy called Hill, whom I had known at Moreton End School, 'captured' them with a pitchfork which he had been using. He had obtained a holiday job on the farm. The Germans put up no resistance and meekly awaited the arrival of the police. I think they were pleased to be out of the war.

I also witnessed an aerial dog fight in the sky between a British Hawker Hurricane and a German bomber. I had been to the Austral cinema that afternoon, despite the lovely sunshine of the early September day. When an air-raid occurred, it was the custom of the cinema to let its audience know by projecting a message onto the screen: "Air-raid in progress. You are advised to take cover." This was communicated by means of an over-projection so that the film was not interrupted. I had promised my mother that if such a message came on the screen, I would leave and quickly go home.

Outside, in Luton Road, I first heard the rat-tat-tat of aerial gunfire and then, against the blue sky, I saw the white silk of a parachute carrying the pilot. A plane overhead, with smoke billowing from its tail, was obviously about to crash somewhere on the Common. I heard later that the plane was a Hawker Hurricane which, in fact, crashed in the field at the end of West Common Way. Its pilot had been the parachutist whom I had seen earlier that afternoon, and I was pleased to hear that he had landed safely. I went the next day to have a look, but souvenir hunting was thwarted by the police who were closely guarding the aircraft to prevent sightseers from getting too near. At the time, it was rumoured that one of the German aeroplanes had also been shot down, but official verification was never made, and I therefore assume that Germany was the victor of that particular skirmish.

Harpenden also had its heroes. Group Captain John "Cats-eyes" Cunningham was a celebrated night fighter pilot and was credited with twelve kills over one fifteen-month period. He was aided only by primitive radar equipment. John Cunningham was one of the most highly decorated air aces during the war, being awarded the Distinguished Service Order (and bar) together with the Distinguished Flying Cross (and bar). For many years he lived at Kinsbourne Green, but sadly died aged eighty five in July 2002.

At about this time, it became a hobby of mine to collect autographs from servicemen who were sporting 'gongs' (or medals) for bravery. I became quite expert in recognising the particular medal ribbon worn, and would ask for an autograph. These were always given, but some were deprecating about the award of medals and were disinclined to speak about the reason for the award. Once, I obtained an autograph from a holder of the Victoria Cross: Corporal Nicholls, whose home town was Nottingham.

Of course, Harpenden also lost some of its sons whilst they were serving their country in the armed forces. I have already mentioned John Lydekker, but another was Robert Nelson, a former captain of cricket at St George's School and, later, a County player. R.P. Nelson led Northants in 1938 and 1939 and, as a left-handed batsman, had been chosen for the aborted MCC tour of India during 1939–40. When he had left St George's School, he and Norman Golds formed a touring club of old boys, called "The Dragons". They came to East Kent. Robert Nelson was killed in 1940 whilst serving as a Royal Marine officer. A seat in his memory can still be seen on Harpenden Common, near the cricket pavilion. The Dragons's touring club still play over the nine days much the same opponents, still under the benevolent command of Mr Golds, even though some sixty years have passed. Another Harpenden man to lose his life was Flying Officer Gavin Morton Sellar (RAFVR), aged twenty-one, the son of Mr and Mrs James Sellar of "Coleswood", East Common. He left a widow, Mrs Jean Sellar.

Early in 1941, we moved home. My father let the flat (No. 3, Bowers House) where we had been living, and sold the main centre part of Bowers House. He rented a small flat, "Kimla", which was on the first floor. The owner, Mr Bertram Jenkins, lived on the ground floor flat and was a 'big noise' at Toynbee Hall. "Kimla" was situated near to the Abbott Anderson factory, on the site now occupied by the fire station. The winter was cold and we had no heating. There were above average snow-falls and I remember trudging with my brother across Leyton Green, singing at the top of our voices, "Good morning, good morning, we've danced the whole night through…" as the snow reached nearly to the tops of our Wellington boots.

In the summer of 1941, when I was thirteen years of age, I got my first holiday job working at Thrales End Farm with my friend, Alan Bell. We were each paid three pence per hour, which is about 1½p in 'decimalised' money. The job, obtained through Alan's mother who knew the farmer's wife, was hard work. The farmer, Mr Piggott, never seemed satisfied with what I did. He was always grumbling and I was as terrified of him as much as if he were my headmaster.

At harvest time, the horse-drawn carts brought along the stooks of wheat. Men perched on the top, then threw them out onto the ground below with their pitchforks. One of my jobs was to get them into line so that the stacking (or 'stooking') could be carried out. I thought I did rather well 'stooking' the wheat into pyramids so that the weather would dry them out, but not to Farmer Piggott's satisfaction. He continually complained that I had no idea how to align the stooks of wheat, nor how to stack them. However, he paid me my meagre wages at the end of the week.

The reaping machine was also horse-drawn and cutting went round the central stand of corn, which got smaller as the reaping progressed. Everyone waited with murderous delight for any poor creature trapped in the middle to break cover. There were rabbits, hares and mice. The farmer and some of his permanent 'hands' armed themselves with shotguns for the final terrified dash of the trapped rabbits and hares. Some escaped but most did not, and made a welcome addition to the farmer's pot during the austerity of the wartime when food was scarce.

There was a wonderful camaraderie when Farmer Piggott was not around. At break-times, my friend and I ate our sandwiches and washed them down with lemonade. The men drank bottles of beer. On fine days, we worked long into the evening to get the harvest in. Sometimes, we all had a sing-song to help the work along.

Although I never worked at Thrales End Farm again, I always got a summer holiday job on one farm or another during the rest of my schooldays – mostly at Claygate apple farm which was situated between the top of Townsend Lane and the 'Nicky' railways. Years later, the farm was purchased by a developer and a housing estate was constructed on its site. Nowadays, Claygate Avenue goes right through the middle of it.

In 1942, we moved home again. This time it was to a typical 1930s semi-detached house on Park Mount (No. 28). In the September, I also went to a new school, travelling to Bedford by train each day. My father also suspended his building business and was appointed D.C.R.C. (Deputy Commander, Royal Engineers), a civilian post in Bedford. He also travelled daily by train (the 7.28 a.m. each morning) but tactfully sat at the opposite end from where my friends and I congregated.

In the Spring of 1943, Harpenden had a new stationmaster. He was Mr W. J. Bland who came from Weedon in Northamptonshire. Mr Bland occupied Station House at the bottom of Station Approach.

Meanwhile, in Harpenden, the streets seemed to be full of members of the armed forces – particularly from the Army, clad in khaki battle-dress and forage caps. There were members of the women's forces too, the A.T.S. girls being employed largely in a secretarial capacity.

A newsletter, published by members of the Comforts Fund Committee, called "Echoes from Harpenden", was specifically for Harpenden men and women serving in H.M. Forces. Anyone killed in action, reported missing, taken prisoner, or, who had been married, promoted, or decorated for gallantry, would eventually appear in the newsletter.

The Salvation Army set up a Forces canteen in my father's joiners' shop at the north end of Bowers House, and facing Dr Blake's old surgery. When my father had sold the main part of

Bowers House, he still retained the flats, outbuildings and yard. This included the large joiners' shop which was converted into the canteen, serving snacks and endless cups of tea at low prices to members of the Forces. Major Mooney of the Salvation Army ran this enterprise. She was already white-haired and very formidable, to say the least. She stood no nonsense from anyone, but she and her staff worked extremely hard. The canteen finally closed in 1946. The showroom of Chirneys Garage (today, the site is occupied by a pizza fast food restaurant next to the George Hotel) was set up as a canteen for A.T.S. girls.

On the site of the present Sainsbury's Supermarket stood the old Broadway Market Hall which was taken over by the Army during the early days of the war, and remained commandeered until after 1945. Pre-war (and again post-war) it was a covered-in market with a wide entrance, and made an ideal headquarters for the Army personnel who used to roar in and out either by motor cycle and side-car, or by jeep. Sometimes, they were transported by the little "Corgis" which were the forerunners of the modern motor scooter. The continuous roar of the motor bikes or "Corgis" must have been distracting to Miss Cooke, whose little sweet shop was at low level on the left-hand side of the entrance. The contrast between the pre-war elegance of Miss Cooke's shop to the hustle and bustle of the Army vehicles was very noticeable.

School life at Bedford was fairly routine. The classrooms were heavily shored up with massive timbers, from floor to ceiling, in case of a bomb attack. Although I was a day-boy, I had to observe the school rules in just the same way as a boarder, although obviously there was not so much close supervision to see that I obeyed them. "Lock-up" was at 6.30 p.m.; that is to say, you were not allowed to be outside your home after this time. We were not permitted to visit any public place of entertainment during term-time, nor to enter Woolworth's or similar store where you would be brought into contact with the public. We were not allowed to eat in the street, nor in public. These were normal school rules, nothing to do with the war. Anyone who was discovered committing any of these offences could be expelled.

Of course, I broke the rules. I went to the cinema in Harpenden at least once a week, sometimes twice. Once, I saw a school monitor inside the foyer; I was convinced that he had been waiting to catch me. The next day, I was summoned to the monitors' room at school, convinced that my expulsion was imminent. All he said was, "The next time you go to the cinema, Webster, for God's sake don't wear your school cap!" I later found out that he had been sitting in the cinema's foyer, waiting for his girl-friend.

The school rules also forbade eating in the railway's buffet on Bedford Station, i.e. a public place, and eating in public generally. Once, I was so hungry after school that I went in for a slab of Maderia cake (price 3 pence or 1½p). I was enjoying this when I suddenly became aware of the Headmaster looking at me through the window. Mr Humphrey Grose-Hodge had sharp eyes and there was no doubt that he had seen me. He probably had an evening engagement in London and was waiting for his train. To his credit, he moved to the other end of the platform and pretended not to have seen me.

Hitler, aggravated by the ingenuity of the British radar defence systems, and furious at the loss of so many aircraft, had decided to postpone his invasion of this island and, disregarding the advice of his senior generals, turned his attention towards Russia. The blunder was to change the face of the war. Added to which, the strength and might of the United States of America entering the war, swung the balance firmly in favour of the allies.

In Harpenden, we heard of the London blitz, the indiscriminate bombings of Coventry and Plymouth, but neither of these events, nor the subsequent V1 and V2 rocket bombs, launched by the Germans, affected Harpenden people directly. The first V1 flying bomb attack on England was launched on 13th June 1944, and the first V2 rocket fell on England on 8th September in the same year.

The trains ran regularly, nearly always to time, and I never remember my train to Bedford being cancelled. Strikes did not occur.

Sometimes, Sir Adrian Boult, the eminent conductor, would travel in my carriage. The BBC Symphony Orchestra used to broadcast from Bedford and I spent many happy hours during rehearsals in the Bedford School Great Hall. I was perched aloft, watching and listening from the second floor gallery to Sir Adrian rehearsing the orchestra well away from the bombing in London. In the evenings, Sir Adrian would travel back to London with some musical score on his lap, which he read like a book.

I recall on one occasion travelling on the train back home to Harpenden dressed in the school's Corps battle-dress uniform. It was a Wednesday and we had 'Corps' all day – marching, drill, map-reading, mile runs carrying full kit on the shoulders. I felt exhausted and, having placed my forage cap in my shoulder epaulette, quickly fell asleep on the train. Nearing Luton, I awoke and saw two elderly ladies sitting opposite. Looking at me, one said to the other: "Isn't it dreadful that they are taking such young boys into the Army nowadays?"

I was about sixteen years of age and she obviously thought that I was a member of H.M. Armed Forces, rather than a member of the school's Corps.

At Batford, a P.O.W. (prisoner of war) camp was set up, mainly to house Italian prisoners. The site of this camp was on the left-hand side of the lane leading to Mackerye End, before reaching "Windmill Cottage". My friends and I used to ride our cycles up the lane to the camp and watch the prisoners behind the fence. They were dressed in dark grey, loose-fitting jackets with the letters "POW" stencilled in white on the back. If we couldn't see any guards, we would jeer: "ITIS, ITIS!"

On Sunday evenings at Harpenden's Public Hall, a variety entertainment was frequently staged for the benefit of the Forces stationed locally. The fun went under the name of "Stars in Battle-dress" and members of the public could also see the show for the price of one shilling (5p) admission. The entertainment was sponsored by ENSA (Entertainments National Service Association) and was excellent value. I remember seeing Terry Thomas – then unknown – and Lieutenant Peter Kavanagh at the Public Hall long before he became a 'star'. Terry Thomas, I recall, was a sergeant and entertained us in a sketch which, years later, he reproduced for television. I still consider Peter Kavanagh ("The Voice of Them All") to be the best impressionist I have ever heard, although his act was more audio than visual, having been brought up to entertain a radio audience. He could reproduce – almost exactly – the voices of many male entertainers of the day and well-known figures, amongst which were Winston

Churchill and Field Marshal Montgomery. These shows certainly cheered up many a Sunday evening when members of the Armed Forces were perhaps feeling rather lonely, away from home.

After the Allies had landed on the Normandy beaches in June 1944, it became more and more obvious that it was only a matter of time before the war would be over. We had maps at home and, daily, pinned little flags on them to plot the position of our troops – the information being gleaned from the morning or evening newspaper.

Eventually, V.E. Day came on 8th May 1945 – Victory in Europe. Celebrations started very early in the morning. Winston Churchill, the Prime Minister, had decreed that it should be a public holiday and I remember seeing soldiers dancing with A.T.S. girls in the High Street as early as 11.00 a.m. Many became drunk but it was a day when no one really cared. I also remember seeing soldiers disappearing into the bushes by the "Prickle Dells", accompanied by their new-found A.T.S. girl friends. Access to the dells could be gained from Walkers Road and was one of the areas on the Common where there was still a good deal of cover to ensure privacy.

At Southdown, a huge bonfire was built on the Green and an "Adolf Hitler" guy was made. He was first hanged, and then put on the bonfire by the school children.

Celebrations went on well into the night and anyone who could play a musical instrument formed, or joined, a four or five-piece band for dancing These were the happy times before the arrival of 'canned' music and its horrible amplification. The night was warm and dry. Open-air dances were held on the Common, at Batford, and on the rugby pitch at the end of Dalkeith Road, now

Let's Dance

It is 1945, the end of the War, and many musicians are still serving in H.M.
Forces. This prompted some of the younger people to form an amateur dance
band. The reverse of the post card (opposite) tells us who's playing – the
author on piano.

the Aldwickbury Crescent estate. People let their hair down and
danced until the small hours of the following day.

The war was over!

Air raids were a thing of the past. Road sign-posts were
reinstated and the blackout, shelters and gas masks became
obsolete overnight. But not so rationing, as Britain struggled
through the peace-time period of bright hope and dull austerity,
and a whole generation of war babies discovered bananas.

Later on in the summer of 1945, Harpenden held its own
victory parade involving Army cadets, sea cadets, A.T.C. cadets,

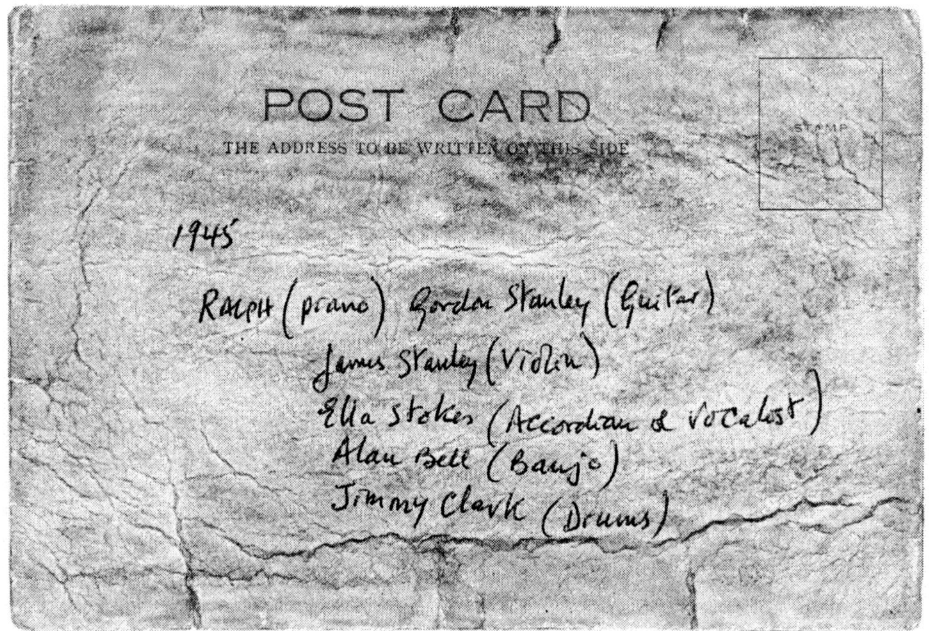

scouts, Homeguard, and other Civil Defence units. They were first amassed in ranks in the area in front of the Public Hall before joining the Grand Parade along the High Street, which was led by the Salvation Army.

At the right-hand side of the Regent Cinema stood an old Victorian house called "The Ancient Lights". It was well-screened from Leyton Road with its garden and perimeter bushes rather overgrown. It was owned by a Mrs Moule and, at the end of the war, she decided to supplement her income – a small pension – by opening a Coffee Lounge, using the large front room for the purpose of seating customers. I think it was the privacy of the place, away from prying eyes, which first attracted the attention and custom of my friends who invited me to have coffee there one morning. It appeared that Mrs Moule had contacts in the U.S.A. who sent her copies of the American "Esquire" magazine. These were liberally scattered round the room for the customers to read. My friends and I had never before read such magazines or seen such daring pictures. For the price of a coffee and scone, we used to spend a couple of hours each morning during the school holiday, reading the magazines and smoking American cigarettes which, by now, were not too difficult to find. These had brand names of "Camel", "Lucky Strike" or "Phillip Morris".

My friends and I were now seventeen years old and grown up. At least, we thought we were.

Books published by
THE BOOK CASTLE

EXPLORING HISTORY ALL AROUND *Vivienne Evans* Planned as seven circular car tours, plus background to places of interest en-route in Bedfordshire and parts of Bucks and Herts.

COUNTRYSIDE CYCLING IN BEDFORDSHIRE, BUCKINGHAMSHIRE AND HERTFORDSHIRE *Mick Payne* Twenty rides on and off-road for all the family.

PUB WALKS FROM COUNTRY STATIONS: Bedfordshire and Hertfordshire *Clive Higgs* Fourteen circular country rambles, each starting and finishing at a railway station and incorporating a pub stop at a mid way point.

PUB WALKS FROM COUNTRY STATIONS: Buckinghamshire and Oxfordshire *Clive Higgs* Circular rambles incorporating pub-stops.

LOCAL WALKS: South Bedfordshire and North Chilterns *Vaughan Basham* Twenty-seven thematic circular walks.

LOCAL WALKS: North and Mid Bedfordshire *Vaughan Basham* Twenty-five thematic circular walks.

FAMILY WALKS: Chilterns South *Nick Moon*
FAMILY WALKS: Chilterns North *Nick Moon*
Two books each containing thirty shorter circular walks.

CHILTERN WALKS: Hertfordshire, Bedfordshire and North Bucks *Nick Moon*
CHILTERN WALKS: Buckinghamshire *Nick Moon*
CHILTERN WALKS: Oxfordshire and West Buckinghamshire *Nick Moon*
A trilogy of collections of circular walks, in association with the Chiltern Society. Each volume contains 30 circular walks.

OXFORDSHIRE WALKS Oxford, the Cotswolds and the Cherwell Valley *Nick Moon*
OXFORDSHIRE WALKS Oxford, the Downs and the Thames Valley *Nick Moon*
Two volumes that complement Chiltern Walks: Oxfordshire, and complete coverage of the county, in association with the Oxford Fieldpaths Society. Thirty circular walks in each.

THE D'ARCY DALTON WAY *Nick Moon* Long-distance footpath across the Oxfordshire Cotswolds and Thames Valley, with various circular walk suggestions.

THE CHILTERN WAY *Nick Moon* The authorised guide to the new 133 mile circular Long-Distance-Path through Bedfordshire, Buckinghamshire, Hertfordshire and Oxfordshire, as planned by the Chiltern Society.

JOURNEYS INTO BUCKINGHAMSHIRE *Anthony Mackay* Superb line drawings plus background text: large format landscape gift book.

COCKNEY KID AND COUNTRYMEN *Ted Enever* The Second World War remembered by the children of Woburn Sands and Aspley Guise.

CHANGING FACES, CHANGING PLACES: Post war Bletchley and Woburn Sands 1945–1970 *Ted Enever* Evocative memoirs of post-war life on the Beds/Bucks borders, up to the coming of Milton Keynes new town.

BUCKINGHAM AT WAR *Pip Brimson* Stories of courage, humour and pathos as Buckingham people adapt to war.

WINGS OVER WING: The Story of a World War 11 Bomber Training Unit *Mike Warth* The activities of RAF Wing in Buckinghamshire.

HISTORIC FIGURES IN THE BUCKINGHAMSHIRE LANDSCAPE *John Houghton*
Major personalities and events that have shaped the county's past, including a special
section on Bletchley Park.

TWICE UPON A TIME *John Houghton* N. Bucks short stories loosely based on fact.

SANCTITY AND SCANDAL IN BEDS AND BUCKS *John Houghton*
A miscellany of unholy people and events.

**MANORS and MAYHEM, PAUPERS and PARSONS: Tales from Four Shires: Beds.,
Bucks., Herts. and Northants** *John Houghton* Little known historical snippets and stories.

BUCKINGHAMSHIRE MURDERS *Len Woodley* Nearly two centuries of nasty crimes.

THE LAST PATROL: Policemen killed on duty while serving the Thames Valley *Len
Woodley*

UNEXPLAINED OXFORD AND OXFORDSHIRE *Marilyn Yurdan* The unexplained
in all its guises in one of the country's most historic towns and the villages of the rest of
the county.

**CHANGES IN OUR LANDSCAPE: Aspects of Bedfordshire, Buckinghamshire and
the Chilterns 1947–1992** *Eric Meadows* Over 350 photographs from the author's
collection spanning nearly 50 years.

JOURNEYS INTO BEDFORDSHIRE *Anthony Mackay* Foreword by The Marquess of
Tavistock, Woburn Abbey. A lavish book of over 150 evocative ink drawings.

FOLK: Characters and Events in the History of Bedfordshire and Northamptonshire
Vivienne Evans Anthology of people of yesteryear – arranged alphabetically by village or
town.

JOHN BUNYAN: His Life and Times *Vivienne Evans* Highly praised and readable
account.

A LASTING IMPRESSION *Michael Dundrow* A boyhood evacuee recalls his years in the
Chiltern village of Totternhoe near Dunstable.

AGAINST THE ODDS: A passion for the country *Michael Dundrow* An intriguing
imaginative sequel to his previous book.

**ELEPHANTS I'LL NEVER FORGET: A Keeper's Life at Whipsnade and London
Zoo** *John Weatherhead* Experiences, dramatic and sad, from a lifetime with these well-
loved giants.

WHIPSNADE MY AFRICA *Lucy Pendar* The inside story of sixty years of this world-
renowned institution. Full of history, anecdotes, and animal stories.

GLEANINGS REVISITED: Nostalgic Thoughts of a Bedfordshire Farmer's Boy
E.W.O'Dell A lively account of rural Bedfordshire in days gone by.

THREADS OF TIME *Shela Porter* The life of a remarkable mother and businesswoman,
spanning the entire century and based in Hitchin and (mainly) Bedford.

HARLINGTON HEYDAYS AND HIGHLIGHTS *Edna L.Wilsher* One of
Bedfordshire's most historic villages, Harlington's yesteryears are seen through the eyes of
one of its most empathetic residents.

FLITWICK: A DAILY TONIC *Keith Virgin* Written as a "Book of Days" containing
extracts from the Flitwick Parish Magazine and local newspapers of around 100 years ago.

FARM OF MY CHILDHOOD, 1925–1947 *Mary Roberts* An almost vanished lifestyle
on a remote farm near Flitwick.

BEDFORDSHIRE'S YESTERYEARS: The Rural Scene *Brenda Fraser-Newstead* Vivid first-hand accounts of country life two or three generations ago.

BEDFORDSHIRE'S YESTERYEARS: Craftsmen and Tradespeople *Brenda Fraser-Newstead* Fascinating recollections over several generations practising many vanishing crafts and trades

BEDFORDSHIRE'S YESTERYEARS: War Times and Civil Matters *Brenda Fraser-Newstead* Two World Wars, plus transport, law and order, etc.

DUNSTAPLELOGIA *Charles Lamborn* Facsimile of a well-respected mid-Victorian town history, with a number of engravings of local buildings.

DUNNO'S ORIGINALS A facsimile of the rare pre-Victorian history of Dunstable and surrounding villages. New preface and glossary by John Buckledee, Editor of The Dunstable Gazette.

DUNSTABLE DOWN THE AGES *Joan Schneider and Vivienne Evans* Succinct overview of the town's prehistory and history – suitable for all ages.

HISTORIC INNS OF DUNSTABLE *Vivienne Evans* Illustrated booklet, especially featuring ten pubs in the town centre.

PROUD HERITAGE: A Brief History of Dunstable, 1000–2000AD *Vivienne Evans* Century by century account of the town's rich tradition and key events, many of national significance.

DUNSTABLE WITH THE PRIORY: 1100–1550 *Vivienne Evans* Dramatic growth of Henry 1's important new town around a major crossroads.

DUNSTABLE IN TRANSITION: 1550–1700 *Vivienne Evans* Wealth of original material as the town evolves without the Priory.

HENRY VIII's DUNSTABLE *Vivienne Evans* Booklet telling of the king's association with the town.

DUNSTABLE DECADE: THE EIGHTIES: A Collection of Photographs *Pat Lovering* A souvenir book of nearly 300 pictures of events in the 1980s.

STREETS AHEAD: An Illustrated Guide to the Origins of Dunstable's Street Names *Richard Walden* Fascinating text and captions to hundreds of photographs, past and present, throughout the town.

DUNSTABLE IN DETAIL *Nigel Benson* A hundred of the town's buildings and features, plus town trail map.

DUNSTAPLE: A Tale of The Watling Highway *A.W.Mooring* Dramatic novelisation of Dunstable's legend of Dunne the Robber – reprinted after a century out of print.

25 YEARS OF DUNSTABLE:. A photographic treasure-trove of the town up to the Queen's Silver Jubilee, 1952–1977 *Bruce Turvey*

DUNSTABLE SCHOOL: 1888–1971 *F.M.Bancroft* Short history of one of the town's most influential institutions.

STRIKE UP THE BAND: Two centuries of music in Dunstable & District *Tony Ward* Visual presentation of the stories behind the many local bands.

BOURNE and BRED: A Dunstable Boyhood Between the Wars *Colin Bourne* Elegantly written, well illustrated book capturing the spirit of the town over fifty years ago.

OLD HOUGHTON *Pat Lovering* Pictorial record capturing the changing appearances of Houghton Regis over the past 100 years.

ROYAL HOUGHTON *Pat Lovering* Illustrated history of Houghton Regis from the earliest of times to the present.

WERE YOU BEING SERVED?: Remembering 50 Luton Shops of Yesteryear *Bob Norman* Well-illustrated review of the much loved, specialist outlets of a generation or two ago.

THE STOPSLEY BOOK *James Dyer* Definitive, detailed account of this historic area of Luton. Includes 150 rare photographs.

THE STOPSLEY PICTURE BOOK *James Dyer* A wealth of new material and photographs make an ideal companion to The Stopsley Book.

PUBS and PINTS: The Story of Luton's Public Houses and Breweries *Stuart Smith* The background to beer in the town, plus hundreds of photographs, old and new.

LUTON AT WAR – VOLUME ONE As compiled by the Luton News in 1947, a well illustrated thematic account.

LUTON AT WAR – VOLUME TWO Second part of the book compiled by The Luton News. New index by James Dyer to both volumes.

THE CHANGING FACE OF LUTON: An Illustrated History *Stephen Bunker, Robin Holgate and Marian Nichols* Luton's development from earliest times to the present busy, industrial town.

WHERE THEY BURNT THE TOWN HALL DOWN: Luton, The First World War and the Peace Day Riots, July 1919 *Dave Craddock* Detailed analysis of a notorious incident.

THE MEN WHO WORE STRAW HELMETS: Policing Luton, 1840–1974 *Tom Madigan* Fine chronicled history, many rare photographs; author served in Luton Police for fifty years.

BARKING MAD: Cautionary Tails! *Danae Johnston* The humorous exploits of two delinquent poodles. A must for dog lovers.

A BRAND NEW BRIGHT TOMORROW . . . A Hatters Promotional Diary *Caroline Dunn* A fans account of Luton Town Football Club during the successful 2001–2002 season.

COMPLETELY TOP HATTERS: Luton Town F.C. – An A–Z of major players, matches and records *Dean Hayes* Stars and incidents throughout the good days and not so good in the club's history.

KENILWORTH SUNSET: A Luton Town Supporter's Journal *Tim Kingston* Frank and funny account of the club's ups and downs.

A HATTER GOES MAD! *Kristina Howells* Luton Town footballers, officials and supporters talk to a female fan.

LEGACIES: Tales and Legends of Luton and the North Chilterns *Vic Lea* Mysteries and stories based on fact, including Luton Town Football Club. Many photographs.

JOURNEYS INTO HERTFORDSHIRE *Anthony Mackay* A foreword by The Marquis of Salisbury, Hatfield House. Introducing nearly 200 superbly detailed line drawings.

STICKS AND STONES: The Life and Times of a Journeyman Printer in Hertford, Dunstable, Cheltenham and Wolverton *Harry Edwards*

SUGAR MICE AND STICKLEBACKS: Childhood Memories of a Hertfordshire Lad *Harry Edwards* Vivid evocation of gentle pre-war in an archetypal village, Hertingfordbury.

CRIME IN HERTFORDSHIRE Volume 1 Law and Disorder *Simon Walker*
Authoritative survey of the changing legal process over many centuries.
CRIME IN HERTFORDSHIRE Volume 2 Murder and Misdemeanours *Simon Walker*
Well researched, detailed murder cases.
BETWEEN THE HILLS: The Story of Lilley, a Chiltern Village *Roy Pinnock* A
priceless piece of our heritage – the rural beauty remains but the customs and way of life
described here have largely disappeared.
THE LILLEY PICTURE BOOK *Betty Shaw* A picture book depicting village activities
during the late nineteenth century and mainly the twentieth century.
HARE AND HOUNDS: The Aldenham Harriers *Eric Edwards* Detailed highly
illustrated history of a countryside institution based in Bedfordshire, Buckinghamshire
and Hertfordshire.
THE HILL OF THE MARTYR: An Architectural History of St.Albans Abbey *Eileen
Roberts* Scholarly and readable chronological narrative history of Hertfordshire and
Bedfordshire's famous cathedral. Fully illustrated with photographs and plans.
MYSTERIOUS RUINS: The Story of Sopwell, St.Albans *Donald Pelletier* Still one of
the town's most atmospheric sites. Sopwell's history is full of fluctuations and interest,
mainly as a nunnery associated with St.Albans Abbey.
HAUNTED HERTFORDSHIRE *Nicholas Connell and Ruth Stratton* Ghosts and other
mysterious occurrences throughout the county's market towns and countryside.
LEAFING THROUGH LITERATURE: Writers' Lives in Herts and Beds *David
Carroll* Illustrated short biographies of many famous authors and their connections with
these counties.
A PILGRIMAGE IN HERTFORDSHIRE *H.M.Alderman* Classic, between-the-wars
tour round the county, embellished with line drawings.
THE VALE OF THE NIGHTINGALE *Molly Andrews* Several generations of a family,
lived against a Harpenden backdrop.
SWANS IN MY KITCHEN *Lis Dorer* Story of a Swan Sanctuary at Hemel Hempstead.
**THE TALL HITCHIN INSPECTOR'S CASEBOOK: A Victorian Crime Novel Based
on Fact** *Edgar Newman* Worthies of the time encounter more archetypal villains.

Specially for Children

VILLA BELOW THE KNOLLS: A Story of Roman Britain *Michael Dundrow* An
exciting adventure for young John in Totternhoe & Dunstable two thousand years ago.
THE RAVENS: One Boy Against the Might of Rome *James Dyer* On the Barton Hills
and in the south-east of England as the men of the great fort of Ravensburgh (near
Hexton) confront the invaders.

Titles acquired by THE BOOK CASTLE

A BEDFORDSHIRE QUIZ BOOK *Eric Meadows* Wide ranging quizzes and picture
puzzles on the history, people, places and bygones of the county.
CURIOSITIES OF BEDFORDSHIRE: A County Guide to the Unusual *Pieter and
Rita Boogaart* Quirky well-illustrated survey of little-known features in the county.

BEDFORDSHIRE WILDLIFE *B.S.Nau, C.R.Boon, J.P.Knowles for the Bedfordshire Natural History Society* Over 200 illustrations, maps, photographs and tables survey the plants and animals of this varied habitat.

THE BIRDS OF BEDFORDSHIRE *Paul Trodd and David Kramer* Environments, breeding maps and details of 267 species, with dozens of photographs, illustrations and diagrams.

THE BIRDS OF HERTFORDSHIRE *Tom Gladwin and Bryan Sage* Essays, maps and records for all 297 species, plus illustrations, photographs and other plates.

THE BUTTERFLIES OF HERTFORDSHIRE *Brian Sawford* History and ecological guide, with colour photographs and maps for nearly 50 species.

WELWYN RAILWAYS *Tom Gladwin, Peter Neville, Douglas White* A history of the Great Northern line from 1850 to 1986, as epitomised by the five-mile stretch between Welwyn Garden City and Woolmer Green. Profusely illustrated in colour and black and white – landscape format.

THE LIFE AND TIMES OF THE GREAT EASTERN RAILWAY (1839–1922) *Harry Paar and Adrian Gray* Personalities, accidents, traffic and tales, plus contemporary photographs and old o.s.maps of this charming railway that transformed East Anglia and Hertfordshire between 1839 and 1922.

THE QUACK *Edgar Newman* Imaginative faction featuring characters in a nineteenth-century painting of a Hitchin market scene – especially quack doctor William Mansell.

D-DAY TO ARNHEIM – with Hertfordshire's Gunners *Major Robert Kiln* Vivid, personal accounts of the D-Day preparations and drama, and the subsequent Normandy battles, plus photographs and detailed campaign maps.

Chiltern Footpath Maps

No.1 High Wycombe and Marlow
No.2 Henley and Nettlebed
No.3 Wendover and Princes Risborough
No.4 Henlet and Caversham
No.5 Sarratt and Chipperfield
No.6 Amersham and Penn Country
No.7 West Wycombe and P.Risborough
No.8 Chartridge and Cholesbury
No.9 The Oxfordshire Escarpment
No.10 Wallingford and Watlington
No.11 The Hambledon Valley
No.12 Hughenden Valley and Great Missenden

No.13 Beaconsfield and District
No.14 Stokenchurch and Chinnor
No.15 Crowmarsh and Nuffield
No.16 Goring and Mapledurham
No.17 Chesham and Berkhamsted
No.18 Tring and Wendover
No.19 Ivinghoe and Ashridge
No.20 Hemel Hempstead and the Gade Valley
No.21 Dunstable Downs and Caddington
No.22 Gerrards Cross and Chalfont St.Peter
No.23 Toddington and Houghton Regis

All the above are available via any bookshop, or from the publisher and bookseller
THE BOOK CASTLE , 12 Church Street, Dunstable, Bedfordshire, LU5 4RU
Tel (01582) 605670   Fax (01582) 662431
Email bc@book-castle.co.uk   Website www.book-castle.co.uk

THE VALE OF THE NIGHTINGALE
Molly Andrews

Over 150 years ago a Romany girl came to work for the squire of Rothamsted Manor in the Hertfordshire village of Harpenden.

So began a fascinating family story spanning six generations there. We follow the life in service and on the farm during the Victorian era – family lore handed down by Molly's mother – and up until the First World War when the author was born.

Molly's insights and anecdotes enlighten us about everyday life and schooldays in the inter-war years. During the depression of the thirties, Molly and her father worked at the famous Rothamsted Agricultural Experimental Station: he was subsequently employed at Vauxhall in Luton.

Two momentous events took place in Molly's life during the early September of 1939. Firstly war was declared on Germany, then her wedding took place – when she carried not only her bouquet but also a gas mask!

Rationing, evacuees, the black-out, munitions-work, the Home Guard, air-raids – all the familiar trials and tribulations of World War 11 are here, enlivened by the first-hand reactions of a typical young couple and all their relatives and friends.

An era ends with the death of the last of the third generation, Molly's mother, in the fifties.

CRIME IN HERTFORDSHIRE
Volume One: Law and Disorder
Volume Two: Murders and Misdemeanours

Simon Walker

Volume One covers the history of law and order in Hertfordshire from the Anglo Saxon period to the middle of the twentieth century. Criminal law, the courts, the punishments and the means of enforcement have changed over the course of more than a thousand years, and the author traces those changes, illustrated with examples drawn from throughout Hertfordshire.

Volume Two is a collection of detailed accounts of crimes drawn from across the county, from 1602 to1939. Locations include Hatfield, Hemel Hempstead, Hoddesdon, Berkamsted, St.Albans, Ware, Hitchin, Datchworth and Bishops Stortford – some of the incidents may be familiar, most will be new to the reader. The rape of Maria Wells by her own father, and the publicity given to her testimony in court, was a tragedy for all concerned. Did Jane Norcott commit suicide, or was it murder? Why did Mary Boddy stab five-year-old George Hitch?

But it is more than just a collection of bloody crime; it provides an insight into the way which many of our Hertfordshire forebears lived their lives.

JOURNEYS INTO HERTFORDSHIRE
Anthony Mackay

This collection of nearly 200 ink drawings depicts the buildings and landscape of the still predominantly rural county of Hertfordshire. After four years of searching, the author presents his personal choice of memorable images, capturing the delights of a hitherto relatively unfeted part of England.

The area is rich in subtle contrasts – from the steep, wooded slopes of the Chilterns to the wide-open spaces of the north-east and the urban fringes of London in the south. Ancient market towns, an impressive cathedral city and countless small villages are surrounded by an intimate landscape of rolling farmland.

The drawings range widely over all manner of dwellings from stately home to simple cottage and cover ecclesiastical buildings from cathedral to parish church. They portray bridges, mills and farmsteads, chalk downs and watery river valleys, busy street scenes and secluded village byways.

The accompanying notes are deliberately concise but serve to entice readers to make their own journeys around this charming county.

HAUNTED HERTFORDSHIRE
A Ghostly Gazetteer
Nicholas Connell and Ruth Stratton

The most extensive collection of the county's ghosts ever written, with over 300 stories. Many are little-known and previously unpublished, having been hidden away in the vaults of Hertfordshire Archives and Local Studies. Others are up to the moment accounts of modern hauntings in the words of those who have experienced them. All supported by dozens of rare and evocative pictures, an outline of the latest theories and diary dates of regular apparition appearances.

Stories feature a feast of phantoms, including grey ladies, dashing cavaliers, spectral transport, headless horsemen and a gallery of Kings and Queens.

Locations include Bishops Stortford, Datchworth, Harpenden, Hertford, Hitchin, Hoddeson, St. Albans, Ware and Watford.

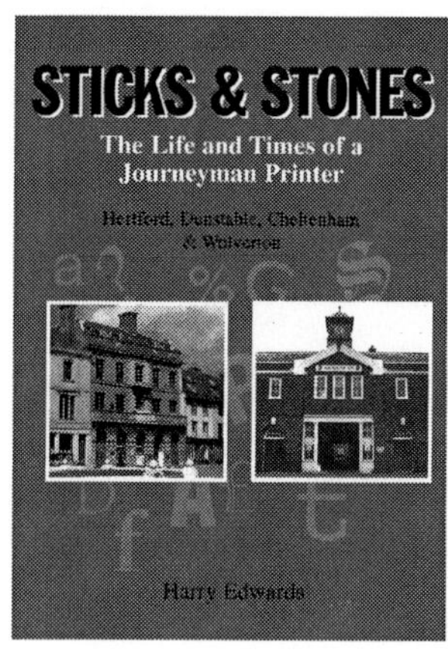

STICKS & STONES
The Life and Times of a Journeyman
Printer Hertford, Dunstable, Cheltenham &
Wolverton
Harry Edwards

Sticks and Stones recounts the story of the author's journey through his life in the printing industry, from printer's devil until retirement. Leaving school at the age of fourteen, Harry's transition from schoolboy to apprentice was abrupt. The journey begins in Hertfordshire, then takes him on to Bedfordshire, Gloucestershire, London and finally to Buckinghamshire. It follows the author's progress as he seeks not only promotion but also the opportunity to become involved in the latest technology, be it cold type composition, photocomposition, or computer-aided typesetting. He touches briefly on his private life when it is appropriate, but the story is primarily about how the changes in the printing industry affected him.

SUGAR MICE AND
STICKLEBACKS
Childhood Memories of a
Hertfordshire Village Lad
Harry Edwards

Memories of a typical English village, Hertingfordbury, in the pre-war days when life was slower and gentler…When the grocer, baker, cobbler, tailor, post-office, sweet-shop and builder's yard were all close at hand; the milk was delivered in a horse drawn cart. Facilities included a village school, a branch-line railway station, a Memorial Hall, a cricket pitch and pavilion, and the imposing Church of St. Mary with its Old Rectory. A vivid picture of country life is conjured up.

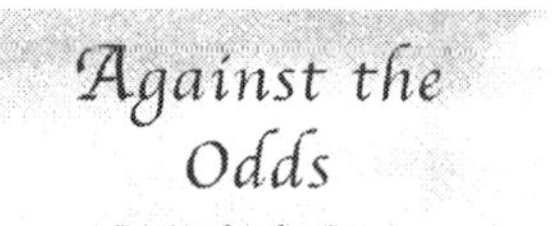

AGAINST THE ODDS
A Passion for the Country
Michael Dundrow

"I can scarcely express with sufficient power and clarity my deep attachment to the people, the life and the surroundings that I came to know and love so much during my evacuation years in the south Bedfordshire village of Totternhoe as described in 'A Lasting Impression'.

"At sixteen I knew well what impotent despair was, as I faced up to the return to East End life after four years on the farm below The Knolls.

"This sequel to that story tells of what might have been, what almost happened in my life in the years that followed the war."

COCKNEY KID AND COUNTRYMEN
The Second World War remembered by the children of Woburn Sands and Aspley Guise
Ted Enever

On the evening of Saturday 7th September 1940, London's East End lay under a pall of smoke from heavy bombing by the German Luftwaffe. It was the beginning of what history was to record as the Blitz.

Six year old Ted and his parents were victims of that first attack. With home and possessions lost, they left London to find safety, shelter and a new way of life in the villages of Woburn Sands and Aspley Guise.

"Cockney Kid and Countrymen" is Ted Enever's story of that new way of life and a snapshot of the wartime years vividly remembered by the village children of the time.

Ted was educated at Bedford Modern School and entered journalism in 1951 with the Bletchley District Gazette. After two years national service he continued his career as a freelance journalist, with various large organisations. On retirement he was working for Milton Keynes Development Corporation. A founder member of the Bletchley Park Trust and now a Patron, Ted is author of "Britains Best Kept Secret – Ultra's base at Bletchley Park."

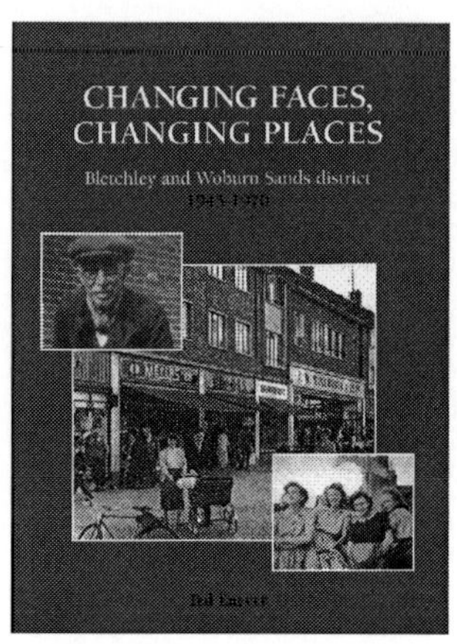

CHANGING FACES, CHANGING PLACES
Bletchley and Woburn Sands district 1945–1970
Ted Enever

'Changing Faces, Changing Places' looks at the 25 year period between the end of the Second World War and the decision to build the new city of Milton Keynes. What occurred then was to turn that part of North Bucks from a collection of small towns and rural villages into the fastest growing urban development in western Europe.

Drawing on the recollections of a wide range of local people, 'Changing Faces, Changing Places' is a sequel to Ted Enever's successful 'Cockney Kid and Countrymen'. From his days travelling by train to Bedford Modern School and through various jobs, particularly as journalist and editor on several local newspapers, it continues the author's own story of life in Aspley Guise, Woburn Sands, Bow Brickhill and Bletchley, told in his own distinctive style.